Darwin and Lady Hope

The Untold Story

Also by L. R. Croft

Handbook of Protein Sequences

Introduction to Protein Sequence Analysis

The Last Dinosaurs

Profitable Beekeeping

Honey and Health

Curiosities of Beekeeping

How Life Began

Allergy to Bee Stings and its Prevention

Honey and Hayfever

The Life and Death of Charles Darwin

Gosse: The Life of Philip Henry Gosse

A Liverpool Family History

Diary of a Naval Commander (as Editor)

A Widow in Paris (as Editor)

Fiction (as Innes Brown)

The Liverpool Venus

Darwin and Lady Hope

The Untold Story

L. R. Croft

Elmwood

First published in Great Britain by Elmwood Books in 2012.

Elmwood Books, 11, Ambleway, Walton-le-Dale, Preston, Lancashire
PR5 4JF

ISBN   978-0-9568089-2-9

Printed and bound by CPI Group (UK) Ltd,
Croydon, CR0 4YY

Contents

"Lady Hope's account of her interview with my father is a fabrication..."

Francis Darwin, 1917

"Lady Hope was not present during his [Darwin's] last illness...I believe he never even saw her. We think the story of his conversion was fabricated in U.S.A. The whole story has no foundation whatever."

Henrietta Darwin, (Mrs Litchfield) 1922

"I do not know how the absurd fiction about my grandfather and Lady Hope ever arose...It is of course, a lie..."

Bernard Darwin, 1928

Preface

I have waited more than twenty years to publish this book, so at the outset I feel it requires some word of explanation. I am not an advocate of conspiracy theories, nor do I have any axe to grind, however I do believe in truth and justice, and this book is concerned with both these virtues.

Almost a quarter of a century ago I became intrigued by the story that Charles Darwin, towards the end of his life, had returned to his earlier Christian faith. I began earnestly to investigate the story and found that it involved an evangelist known as 'Lady Hope', however, no one seemed to be able to identify this lady. Most of the authorities I consulted referred to her as a 'myth', or else 'a shadowy figure' and claimed that the whole story was a fabrication, a falsehood and a malicious lie. I was, however, undaunted and pursued my investigations and eventually I was able to identify the lady as indeed a real person. She was Elizabeth Lady Hope, the daughter of General Sir Arthur Cotton, and the widow of the Admiral of the Fleet, Sir James Hope of Carriden. This discovery made the story more plausible, for why should a person with this distinguished background fabricate a story about Charles Darwin. I decided my findings were important enough to deserve a wider audience so I wrote an article on the subject and submitted it to the leading scientific journal *Nature*, but needless to say, I received a sharp rebuff from its editorial team. Looking back it is clear that I was being a bit naive and this became more obvious to me some months later when I published my findings in a book. This was published in May 1989 and had the title, *The Life and Death of Charles Darwin*. Although like any author I expected a certain degree of criticism, I was unprepared for the nasty personal attacks that I received. I believed I had embarked on a search for the truth, but in reality I had opened up a can of worms and unleashed the forces of historical distortion. Now looking back at my experience I can appreciate the words of Robert Louis Stevenson's famous dictum namely: "It must always be foul to tell what is false but it can never be safe to suppress what is true."

So what then is the truth of the story?

The year 2009 marked the bicentenary celebrations of the birth of Charles Darwin and many publishers brought out new Darwin books, and reprints. Among the many books issued was a book on Darwin's religious views, published by a long-established Christian publishing house. In the opening pages the author confidently claimed that despite rumours to the contrary Charles Darwin did not convert to Christianity in the months before his death in the April of 1882.

Following a careful study of the book I was intrigued to know why the author had failed to mention Lady Hope's claim that Darwin had indeed regained his faith, and accordingly I wrote to the author, by way of his publisher, and enclosed a complimentary copy of my book. I then waited, and waited, but received no reply. I felt that this was unusual, as publishers usually encourage their authors to respond to readers who have purchased their books. I then wrote again to the publisher, and in a reply it was confirmed that my query and my book had been forwarded to the author, but I have still not received any response. Surprisingly, his editor also was not prepared to reply to my question. This episode impressed on me just how deep-seated was the belief that Lady Hope's account was false and fraudulent. So effective has been this character assassination that sadly any casual search of the internet today will turn up hundreds of web-pages that condemn Lady Hope to be a liar, a fraudster and a hoaxer.

The origin of this mischief goes back to the early part of the last century when the Darwin family, together with their supporters, promoted their gilded image of Darwin as the honourable unbeliever. Thus when Lady Hope gave her version of Darwin's religious views it was vehemently denied and she was savagely attacked, and was eventually hounded out of the country and forced to live in exile in the United States.

Today, I cannot believe that the woman who was admired for her integrity by Lord Shaftesbury, and praised by Florence Nightingale for her generous humanitarianism, could be thought of as inventing a story about Darwin to satisfy her own vanity. For that reason I believe that the results of my twenty-year search for the truth should be published and the facts made known. I hope I have looked at the evidence objectively and so reached the historical truth. I make no apology about the fact that this book is more about Lady Hope than it is about Charles Darwin. But it is Lady Hope's reputation that has been destroyed and it is her memory that has been denigrated. I believe it is now time for some justice to be done and that her good name be restored, and that is the ultimate purpose of this book. It is now more than twenty years since I set off on this journey to prove that what I had written in my biography of Darwin was true. I believe that the discoveries now described not only substantiate my previous claims, but more importantly they vindicate the good name and character of Elizabeth Lady Hope.

L.R. Croft   15 January 2012

Chapter 1

A Strange Coincidence

One morning in June 1858 Charles Darwin picked up the morning post. Among his letters was a thin package that had travelled thousands of miles from a small island in the Dutch East Indies near New Guinea, called Ternate. At this time he had built up a large number of correspondents around the world who would send him specimens, or else, provide him with useful information, but on this occasion he was mystified as to the identity of his correspondent. On opening the package he discovered it was from Alfred Russel Wallace, a fellow naturalist whom he had asked to send him items of interest from South East Asia where he was travelling. Darwin on reading the enclosed letter expected to read of some unusual creature, or observation, instead, what he read was to change his life for ever. Enclosed with the letter was a short handwritten manuscript that outlined the same theory of evolution by natural selection, as he himself had devised, but had not yet published. What appeared remarkable to Darwin was that Wallace had repeated all of the same ideas as he had come to, and had reached the same argument completely independently. Darwin was completely shocked, 'I never saw a more striking coincidence,' he wrote, 'if Wallace had my MS sketch written out in 1842 he could not have made a better short abstract.'

A strange coincidence, indeed, but here is another one. Some years ago, I published a biography of Darwin entitled, *The Life and Death of Charles Darwin*. It was only a short book, and for some unknown reason, I went to a disproportionate length to discuss Darwin's consanguineous marriage to his cousin, Emma Wedgwood, and put forward my idea that Darwin's ill-health had been exacerbated by anxiety arising from his realisation that by marrying his cousin he had contributed to the ill-health of his children. I wrote that Darwin, "lived in constant fear that he had, by marrying his cousin, enhanced the likelihood that the Darwin family illness would be passed on to his children....These dark thoughts must have deepened his gloom and despondency."

Since that time several other writers have developed this idea,[1] but at the time, I was the only one to have put it forward. Furthermore, at that time, I did not know that Darwin's awareness of the problem had come about on his reading Anthony Trollope's novel, *The Small House at Allington*, which had been published in the *Cornhill Magazine* in 1862. It is one

---

[1] Adam Kuper, Commentary: A Darwin family concern, *Int.J.Epidemiology*,(2009) 39, p.1439 ; J. Leake, Unnatural selection: Darwin's family damaged by inbreeding, *Sunday Times*, May,2, (2010)

readers consider to be Trollope's finest novel. It has a complex plot with numerous sub-plots but it could be described as a family saga. One of its themes is marriage and inheritance, a subject always of interest to Darwin. But what must have made him sit up, as he listened to his wife, Emma, reading it out loud, was when Lord De Guest of Guestwick Manor mentions to his new doctor about one of the young Dale girls.

"A very pretty girl she is, too. I remember seeing her at her uncle's last year. I shouldn't wonder if she were to marry her cousin Bernard."

The young doctor then replied:

"I'm not quite sure that it's a good thing for cousins to marry."

The doctor's name? It was a Dr. Croft. A strange coincidence? Possibly.

But strange coincidences do occur.

In the novel, *A Certain Justice*, the crime writer P. D. James has her main character Venetia Aldridge QC musing about an incident outside her home when she concludes: "Had it been a coincidence? Strange ones had happened. You couldn't be a criminal lawyer without encountering almost weekly the capricious phenomenon of chance."

Do we immediately jump to the conclusion that someone is being dishonest when we feel their story is unlikely. Take for instance, the encounter of a young lady and a depressed doctor on a railway platform, late on a summer's afternoon around the year 1873, somewhere in the south of England. She has been busy all day reading the Bible to sick people in the villages. He notices her Bible in her hand and confesses he has lost all faith. They go their separate ways. She then remembers where she had seen him before and is determined to visit him and talk about the gospel, but before she is able to do so, he kills himself. A strange coincidence, or a pious fib? It is easy to ridicule it and assume that it is the latter. But we could be wrong.

And then there is the story of the eminent scientist approaching the end of his life. He has devoted all his life to developing a theory of the world that does away with the need for God. He is like the doctor on the railway platform, he lives in a world that lacks purpose and meaning, but then on seeing the young lady with her Bible it rekindles a spark of hope, and he grasps out for the faith he once had. An unlikely story? Perhaps. But then strange coincidences do occur, so are we right to assume that it is all a tall story?

This is what this book is about. The eminent scientist is Charles Darwin and the young woman is the evangelist Lady Hope. Is her story simply a pious fable, or has she told the truth? It is easy to ridicule the story, and many have. For almost a century her existence was declared a 'mystery', or a 'shadowy figure', and others claimed it was a 'myth', she was an 'hallucination', or it was all a 'fabrication'. The Darwin family made out that it had all been started in America. Then when Lady Hope was found to have been a real person, and may indeed have visited Darwin, her character was subject to vicious and malicious gossip so as to destroy her credibility.

In this book I hope to uncover the truth. It has taken much research delving into archives across the country, and searching the shelves of secondhand bookshops, but at last I believe I have found the solution to this mystery.

Chapter 2

The Brief Encounter

In 1945, the British film, *Brief Encounter*, was released, in which the actors Celia Johnson and Trevor Howard played the principal parts. The film had been based on a stage play by Noel Coward, that was entitled, *Still Life*. This had been first produced in 1936. Since its release, the film has won numerous awards and has been shown on television, so many times, that its plot is familiar to everyone. So it is only necessary to draw attention to the fact that the story involves a casual meeting, on a railway platform, of a young lady and a doctor.

Some fifty years before a similar story had been published in a little known work entitled, *Heavenly Blossoms On Earth's Pathway*. The story also involves a casual meeting between a young lady and a doctor on a railway platform, but the author's purpose in writing the story, was a world away from that of Noel Coward. The author was the evangelist, Lady Hope, who had been born in Tasmania on, December 9, 1842, and she published the story in 1899. This is her story:

"I was standing at a country station late on a summer afternoon, watching for the arrival of a friend by the six o'clock train. Beside me there stood a few other people, also waiting for the same train. A gentleman greeted me, whom I did not recognise. I suppose I looked hot and tired after a very busy day, for he said to me, 'You have been hurried in trying to be here on time.'

I said, 'Yes, I have been very busy for several hours amongst the people, visiting from house to house.'

He said, 'You are always busy, are you not?'

'Oh!' I replied, 'my life is so full of interest! It is such a joy to be able to take to the people the message of Christ's love and mercy.'

'You believe in Him?' he asked.

'Believe in Him!' I said. 'Do you not believe in Him? He is all in all to me.'

'I am not sure of anything,' he replied. 'I have no beliefs at all now, for I do not know what is true and what is not true. Life is an entire mystery, and a very sad one, I think.'

He spoke in such a serious tone, in a very low voice, so that even in the little crowd standing round us, no one could hear him but myself.

At this point we were interrupted by the arrival of the train, and I wondered to myself who my acquaintance could be, for I had not the slightest recollection of ever having seen him before. However, as we drove away from the station, I remembered that he was a doctor, a comparatively young man, residing in a house of one of our friends, a gentleman whom we knew very well, and whose state of health was such that he considered it advisable always to have this trusted man with him whilst in the country: and I inwardly resolved there and then that I would very soon find an opportunity of going to the house, when I might have another conversation with the gentleman who had so interested me a few minutes before...

I never saw him again.

The next morning he did not come down to breakfast. They waited for him some time. As ten o'clock struck they became anxious, and sent a servant to his room. The reply was that the door was locked, and that he had knocked several times, but there was no reply.

The report spread in the house that something must have occurred, and the gardener procured a ladder and climbed in the window. Here he entered the room and found, to his horror, that the doctor had drawn a chair in front of the looking glass and deliberately cut his throat, thus, as he considered, putting an end to the existence of a miserable life! But was it the end? Let us ask ourselves this question.

He had left a note on the table, written only three hours after his confession to me of his miserable state of mind, his uncertainties, and his non-belief."[2]

This account has been partially reproduced in the book, *Evangelicals and Science in Historical Perspective*, by the historian James Moore as an example of how the evangelist Lady Hope had used the same "well worn idiom" in this account as she had in her published report of Darwin's conversion, and that both stories were untrue, indeed he claimed them to be "brilliant counterfeits". He further concluded that it was not her first effort of self-aggrandizement. "In Britain she had honed her anecdotal skills in dozens of books and tracts. Her embroidery was exquisite, colouring her own good deeds, appealing to pious sentiment. The Darwin anecdote was only her latest life-and-death 'true story'"[3]

However, Moore had been very selective in which parts of this particular account he used. On examination, one finds

---

[2] Lady Hope, *Heavenly Bloosoms on Earth's Pathway*, pp. 68-71.
[3] James Moore, *Evangelicals and Science in Historical Perspective* (ed. D.N.Livingstone, D.G.Hart, and M.A.Noll) p.225-226

that he missed out a very important paragraph, which has also been deliberately omitted above, it follows on from the ellipsis, and is:

"When I went home, I related what had passed to my parents, and remarked: 'We must have that young man on the right side; he is so earnest and thoughtful, it would be a grand thing if he could learn to believe.'"

In other words, there were witnesses to her story, her mother and father, both of whom were devout Christians. They would have read her book, and would have recalled such a tragic incident as this, as indeed would other local people. In the Preface, Lady Hope makes clear that the stories recorded in the book are all true, "I have published some of the incidents which have happened to myself in that daily experience..." there is no way therefore that she could have fabricated this story without risking bringing into question her integrity. But aside from this, there is a much more significant feature, and again it was omitted by Moore. It is the paragraph that follows on from the extract given above, it reads:

"An impression was left upon my mind from this terrible occurrence that can never be effaced, and has only helped to confirm the strong feeling I have always had of the intense sadness of a life spent without God; and I only insert this tragic little history, <u>much against my own inclination,</u> (*my emphasis*) that I may emphasise the despairing misery that can take possession of a mind that has not the rest of saving faith and the gift of that 'peace which passeth all understanding.'"

In other words, even after many years, this "terrible occurrence" still affected her, and in fact she was so strongly affected by it that she did not really want to relate it in public. This is not what one would have expected if the story had been fabricated. It is too much to believe that she would also go on and feign emotional upset. Thus the only reasonable conclusion is that it was a completely true story, and not some sort of fable as claimed by Professor Moore.

The mistake Professor Moore has made is in lacking an appreciation of the sort of life Lady Hope had. As is made clear in her story, when she tells the doctor, "I have been very busy...visiting from house to house...my life is so full of interest". She didn't sit at home all day, she had followed her father's advice, who had told her: "Do something, my girl, do something. Never be idle for a single moment. Remember, Time is short, Eternity is near." So, she was out and about, Bible reading, hospital visiting, helping the poor and sick, and spreading the gospel to coal miners, navvies and lime pit workers. At this time, female evangelists were not hesitant at talking to strangers, as their approach would not usually be misinterpreted. Furthermore, decorum did not require a chaperon, when they spoke, or prayed, alone with a person. With such a life, exceptional incidents did occur, and meeting the depressed doctor on the station platform that day was just one of them, albeit a terrible one. Indeed, it is what P. D. James has called: "the capricious phenomenon of chance"[4].

---

[4] "You couldn't be a criminal lawyer without encountering almost weekly the capricious phenomenon of chance." P. D. James, *A Certain Justice*, p.54

Chapter 3

The Darwin Legend

Charles Darwin is today a national icon, but not everyone would go so far as a recent editorial in *The Times* newspaper which suggested that he has, 'a plausible claim to be counted the greatest figure in this nation's history'. Nevertheless, it is a fact that more books have been written about him than any other scientist. How Darwin has achieved this distinction remains a mystery, but what is remarkable is the fact that he himself maintained that he had only modest intellectual ability. The fact that he is now an archetypal Victorian is remarkable, so much so, that there have been attempts to make his home at Down House in Kent become a World Heritage site.

The year 2009 was important as it marked the bicentenary of his birth and throughout the land there were celebrations and exhibitions. *The Times* on, Thursday 12 February, printed a special edition to mark the occasion. The year was also marked by the publication of numerous books, and new editions of Darwin's writings, so that the shelves in many bookshops began to weaken under the increased weight. Yet, in all these publications, exhibitions, celebrations, television and radio programmes, the message was clear and unanimous, namely that although Darwin had at one time been a candidate for the ministry in the Anglican church, he had rejected that faith, and had died an agnostic. There had been no repentance and no deathbed, or any other, conversion. Any such claim was a fabrication, and totally malicious and mendacious.

Thus we read in Professor Tim Berra's book, *Charles Darwin: The Concise Story of an Extraordinary Man*, published by John Hopkins University Press, at Baltimore, which is the oldest university press in North America, that the suggestion that Darwin may have returned to the Christian faith, was "a fraud". The professor then went on to refer his readers to James Moore's book, *The Darwin Legend* for "a full exposition of this fraud". And in *Darwin's Notebook*, by Jonathan Clements, and published by The History Press, the suggestion of Darwin's conversion, was "a hoax" and the hoaxer was Lady Hope. It was, the author declared, "Hope's Hoax". Then, in *Galileo Goes To Jail*, published by Harvard University Press, Professor James Moore, writes a chapter entitled, "Myth 16: That evolution destroyed Darwin's faith in Christianity until he reconverted on his deathbed," in which he claimed that the Darwin conversion story was "a brilliant counterfeit" that had been promoted by "untutored evangelicals".

It is clear that the denigration of Lady Hope's reputation has rested on the opinion of Professor James Moore, of the Open University. Moore is the co-author of a major biography of Darwin that was published in 1991. What is strange is that in this 800-page biography there is no mention of Darwin's alleged conversion, neither is there any reference to Lady Hope, despite the fact that Moore claims to have spent the previous twenty years researching the Darwin-Lady Hope incident. However, he did publish an addendum to his major tome, albeit this time, somewhat surprisingly, without his co-author. This was entitled, *The Darwin Legend*, and it was published in 1995. In this book, Moore accepts the fact that Lady Hope did visit Darwin in the autumn of 1881, however he could not accept the content of their discussion as told by Lady Hope. Significantly, he had no evidence to suggest that Lady Hope's claims were false, other than basing his opinion on a general distaste for evangelical Christianity.

But he is not alone. The atheist, Richard Dawkins has similar feeling towards the Lady Hope story and in a television interview has stated that it is a "complete lie".[5]

Thus Lady Hope's report of Darwin's conversion, was "a hoax", "a fraud", "a brilliant counterfeit" and that Lady Hope

---

[5] Richard Dawkins on the Bill Maher Show, June 21, 2011.

was completely dishonest and a downright liar. But was she? And what was the evidence? Certainly none of the above authors had provided any evidence to support such a serious allegation. In the event I wrote to Harvard University Press, and in turn, lawyers acting for them made clear their position. In a letter I received from them, it was stated that:

"In any event the ordinary reader would consider that Professor Moore's conclusion is that Lady Hope falsified her story."

For an author to accuse someone, in print, of dishonesty, or that they are a liar, is not a step to be taken lightly. Besides the serious legal implications, one has to be completely certain of one's facts, otherwise one's own reputation is at risk.

The legal position is clear, as outlined by Mr Justice Jacob in the Court of Appeal, he stated:

"The standard of proof is the ordinary civil standard, namely a balance of probabilities. On the other hand it is well-established that a civil court when considering a charge of fraud will naturally require for itself a higher degree of probability than that which it would require for a lesser test. The reasons for that were articulated by Lord Nicholls. Essentially the point is that one does not set out assuming that people are dishonest. Fortunately most people are not dishonest. So, to find somebody dishonest is therefore to find that they have acted very differently from the ordinary citizen. Proof of fraud therefore requires evidence good enough to overcome a strong presumption of innocence."[6]

In other words, in English law, civil claims involving fraud, demand a higher criteria of evidence. Normally, in civil litigation it is 'the balance of probability', but in cases of fraud it is raised to the higher standard of, 'beyond reasonable doubt'. Therefore, for someone to accuse Lady Hope of fraud, or dishonesty, they would need very strong evidence so as to exclude any reasonable doubt. But the truth is, none of the above authors have produced any evidence that Lady Hope was dishonest. None at all. The allegations made against her are derived purely from prejudice against any form of evangelical Christianity. The truth is, these authors shudder at the possibility that Darwin may have embraced Christianity in the last months of his life.

Further insight into this matter may be obtained from looking at how Professor Moore has treated Lady Hope's father, General Sir Arthur Cotton. General Cotton spent some forty years of a distinguished army career in India, where he supervised the construction of the gigantic irrigation projects

---

[6] Mr Justice Jacob, Parks v. Clout [2003] EWCA Civ 893.

across the Godavari River. This work resulted in saving millions of people from the famines that had previously ravaged the area. Today, General Cotton's name is revered in India, and numerous statues have been erected to his memory. In fact, he is the only Englishman to have had a statue erected to his memory, by the Indian people, since Independence. Furthermore, there is today a Sir Arthur Cotton Museum in the State of Andhra Pradesh, and the recently constructed dam across the Godavari River has been named the 'Sir Arthur Cotton Barrage' in his memory. In addition to all these honours, the Jawaharlal Nehru Technological University has recently planned the making of a documentary film about Sir Arthur Cotton's life and work.

In contrast, Professor Moore has given a rather different version of Lady Hope's father. In his book, *The Darwin Legend*, Moore states that General Sir Arthur Cotton was, "the man who wrung more revenue out of the Madras plantations than any previous administrator"[7].

General Cotton was an evangelical Christian who spent his life working for the good of others, and this is evident from the way his memory is respected. Shortly after his death in 1899, Major-General Haig in a letter to *The Times* referred to him as " a great man whose works have conferred untold benefits upon

---

[7] J. Moore, *The Darwin Legend*, p.44

the people of India".[8] He has also been referred to as: "The greatest engineering genius India has ever known".[9] Moore's comment is surprising as it is totally inaccurate. However, it clearly demonstrates that he is antagonistic to the evangelical Christian. Consequently, this must bring into question his opinion as to the Darwin-Lady Hope story. On this account, in the pages that follow the background to the dispute will be re-considered from which reasonable and objective conclusions will be sought.

---

[8] Cf. *The Times*, Thursday, January 3, 1901, p.9.
[9] *Jackson's Oxford Journal*, Saturday, August 26, 1899.

Chapter 4

The Lady Hope Story

Professor Janet Browne of Harvard University has studied the changing representation of Darwin in biographies published since his death in 1882.[10] She has correlated many of these to sociological and political changes of the time. In the early biographies the image given of him was that derived from what the Darwin family had released to the public. This was largely from notes Darwin had left in the form of a private autobiography, together with selective correspondence. The image that resulted was of a Darwin that was a good, honest and decent family man, who had devoted his life to the study of natural history while suffering great pain and illness. He was made out to be a very modest man with moderate opinions on both politics and religion. He was a decent magistrate, and supported the local parish church as well as certain missionary societies. He was certainly never anti-Christian. This image of Darwin is repeated in most of the early biographies, and is most clearly seen in Robert Cochrane's short biography published in

---

[10] Janet Browne, *Journal of Interdisciplinary History*, (2010) pp.347-373

1888, shortly after Darwin's death.[11] Thus we read that Darwin was 'patient in observation and analysis' and 'for forty years led a quiet life devoted to science'. He took 'great delight in his children' and visitors found in him 'a model host'. He was 'a diligent naturalist' whose great work was, 'accomplished by a man who almost constantly was in a state of health little removed from that of an invalid'. This latter claim is perpetuated in many biographies, and represents the glamorisation of his ill-health as being the penalty for serious intellectual pursuit.

Unfortunately, this early view of Darwin which is largely derived from private notes, intended only for his family, has provided an effective barrier to understanding the real man. One author has recently concluded that, 'uncritical reliance' on the autobiography, 'has produced a distorted picture'[12]. Indeed Janet Browne as gone so far as to state that Darwin's autobiography was 'an exercise in camouflage', and that the real Darwin was a person 'resolutely private'. Thus it is only now that researchers are coming to the conclusion that Darwin excluded his innermost thoughts from his family, so that even his wife Emma, did not really know what he thought.

---

[11] Cochrane, R., *Great Thinkers and Workers*, pp210-233.
[12] Secord, J.A., *British Journal History of Science*, (1991), pp.133-157.

These difficulties will be referred to later. It is much easier at this stage to summarize the basic facts concerning his life. He was born on, February 12, 1809 at the small market town of Shrewsbury in Shropshire. His father was Robert Darwin, a successful physician, and his mother was Susannah Wedgwood, the daughter of Josiah Wedgwood, the founder of the famous pottery company. Darwin was intended to follow his father into medicine and was sent to study in Edinburgh, however he dropped out, and was sent to Cambridge University to train for the ministry in the Anglican church. Darwin's ambition at the time was to follow in the footsteps of Gilbert White, and become a country parson and engage in the study of natural history. However he was offered the opportunity to travel around the world, on a surveying voyage aboard HMS *Beagle*, under the command of Robert FitzRoy. The voyage would take five years and on his return he wrote up his experiences and natural history observations which when published established him, almost overnight, to be a leading naturalist.

On January 29, 1839 he married his first cousin Emma Wedgwood at St Peter's church, Maer. At first they lived in London but on account of the dreadful pollution in the city they moved out in September 1842 to live in the small village of

Downe, in Kent. The house they settled in was called Down House. It was a large Georgian building that had once been a parsonage. It was here that Darwin continued his natural history studies and with his wife brought up a large family.

Over the following years Darwin continued with his natural history studies, and formulated his evolution theory, while at the same time he slowly abandoned his religious beliefs. His theory was eventually published in November 1859, in his book entitled, *On the Origin of Species by means of Natural Selection.* Its publication created uproar as the concept of a godless origin of species challenged the Church and the religious faith of many.

In June 1860, the evolution theory was debated at the British Association meeting at Oxford, when it met at the Natural History Museum. Darwin was not present but remained in seclusion at Down. In his place was Thomas Henry Huxley, later to be known as 'Darwin's bulldog'. During the debate the Bishop of Oxford, Samuel Wilberforce challenged Huxley and demanded of him whether he was descended from an ape on his grandmother, or his grandfather's side. The audience reacted immediately with laughter, but Huxley remained calm and replied that he would rather be descended from a humble ape than from an educated man who abused his considerable gifts and position by denying the truth and ridiculing a serious scientific discussion. The upshot was mayhem, and it is recorded that one lady fainted, but hundreds got up and cheered him.

However, Darwin had never denied the existence of God. Although he had been brought up an Anglican, over the years he had given up his beliefs, and was happy to call himself an agnostic. Nevertheless, he was strongly attached to the parish church, and was friendly with the local vicar. He had all his children baptised in the church, and he supported missionary charities. On the other hand, his wife was religious she was a Unitarian, and attended the parish church together with their children.

For most of his life Darwin suffered from poor health. It is possible he had contracted Chagas disease during expeditions in South America, but it is also likely his illness had a psychosomatic component. Towards the end of his life he developed heart problems which eventually led to a fatal heart attack on, April 19, 1882. Thus he had been aware of the serious nature of his illness, and had in fact informed one of his friends that he had "received his warning". It is therefore not surprising that at this time he might have turned to the Bible and sought a renewal of his youthful faith. However, there is very little in his published work, or correspondence that supports the view that he may have done so. However, the Darwin family have been exceptionally vigorous in promoting their image of Darwin as an unbeliever, that it cannot be ruled out that documents suggesting otherwise may have been destroyed.

It was only some years after his death that evidence came to light that he had returned to a belief in the Christian faith. One of the first reports was printed in the *Boston Evening Transcript* of Saturday August, 21, 1915. It was in the religious section of the newspaper under the heading, "Darwin and Christianity", it announced, "A remarkable story told of the great scientist and author when he was approaching the end of earthly life", and in a footnote the report stated that Lady Hope 'a consecrated English woman' had related the story at a morning prayer meeting, at the annual conference at the Northfield College, Massachusetts, just a few days before[13]. The story had then been repeated from the platform by Professor A.T. Robertson, an eminent New Testament scholar. Lady Hope's story was as follows:

"It was on one of those glorious autumn afternoons that we sometimes enjoy in England when I was asked to go in and sit with the well-known professor, Charles Darwin. He was

---

[13] The Northfield College was a girls' college founded by the evangelist, Dwight L. Moody

almost bedridden for some months before he died. I used to feel when I saw him that his fine presence would make a grand picture for our Royal Academy: but never did I think so more strongly that on this particular occasion.

He was sitting up in bed, wearing a soft embroidered dressing gown of rather a rich purple shade. Propped up by pillows he was gazing out on a far-stretching scene of woods and cornfields, which glowed in the light of one of those marvellous sunsets which are the beauty of Kent and Surrey. His noble forehead and fine features seemed to be lit up with pleasure as I entered the room.

He waved his hand toward the window as he pointed out the scene beyond while in the other hand he held an open Bible which he was always studying.

"What are you reading now," I asked as I seated myself by his bedside.

"Hebrews!" he answered – "still Hebrews, 'The Royal Book' I call it. Isn't it grand?"

Then placing his finger on certain passages he commented on them.

I made some allusion to the strong opinions expressed by many persons on the history of the Creation, its grandeur and then their treatment of the earlier chapters of the Book of Genesis.

He seemed greatly distressed, his fingers twitched nervously, and a look of agony came over his face as he said:

"I was a young man with unformed ideas. I threw out queries, suggestions wondering all the time over everything; and to my astonishment the ideas took like wildfire. People made a religion of them."

Then he paused and after a few more sentences on "the holiness of God" and "the grandeur of this Book" looking at the Bible which he was holding tenderly all the time, he suddenly said:

"I have a summer-house in the garden, which holds about thirty people. It is over there," pointing through the open window. "I want you very much to speak there. I know you read the Bible in the villages. Tomorrow afternoon I should like the servants on the place, some tenants, and a few of the neighbours to gather there. Will you speak to them?"

"What shall I speak about?" I asked.

"Christ Jesus" he replied in a clear emphatic voice, adding in a lower tone, "and his salvation. Is not that the best theme? And then I want you to sing some hymns with them. You lead on your small instrument do you not?"

The wonderful look of brightness and animation on his face as he said this I shall never forget, for he added :

"If you take the meeting at three o'clock this window will be open and you will know that I am joining in with the singing."

How I wished that I could have made a picture of the fine old man and his beautiful surroundings on that memorable day!"

The account reprinted above is as it appears in the Boston newspaper. It had been published by permission of the editor of the Baptist journal the *Watchman-Examiner*, in which it had first appeared some days before. Since that time it has been reprinted many times in numerous newspapers and journals. In the above account the identity of the 'consecrated English lady' was given as Lady Hope, but in some other reprints her identity was not given. In the following chapter the reaction to the publication of Lady Hope's remarkable story will be considered.

Chapter 5

Reaction to the Lady Hope Story

When Lady Hope's story reached England it was in the autumn of 1915. Britain had been at war with Germany for more than a year and thousands of lives had been lost. People were now living beneath the shadow of all-out-war, and no one was exempt from the dire consequences. Under these circumstances, the reports in American newspapers as to what Darwin might have said on his deathbed, attracted little attention. In wartime, people are more, not less religious, so Darwinism had not yet been absorbed, to any great extent, by the British population.

Meanwhile the Darwin family were intent on promoting their sanctified image of Darwin as the good and noble unbeliever. Indeed, it was crucial for them to promote this version of Darwin in order to ensure that his ideas would become acceptable. One needs to remember that at this time, atheism was still frowned upon in respectable society. It was only a few years before that the atheist, and elected member of parliament, Charles Bradlaugh, had been excluded from taking his seat in the House on account of his lack of belief, and concern over the potential outrage that would result from him taking the oath on the Bible.

In the event, Darwin's third son, Francis, took up the challenge and firmly responded. He had edited the *Life and Letters of Charles Darwin*, which had been published in 1887. This promoted the respectable and authoritative picture of Darwin, which the family wanted to establish. The possibility that this image might now be distorted by Lady Hope's claims convinced them that immediate action was necessary. The story had to be smothered at birth. Francis Darwin's first action was to write to the editors of the journals that had printed the story and to make clear to them that Lady Hope's story was untrue. In a letter dated, 8 November 1915, he wrote to Professor A.T. Robertson and stated:

"Neither I nor other members of my family have any knowledge of Lady Hope and there are almost ludicrous points in her statement which make it impossible to believe that she ever visited my father at Down....I regret that you should have been misled into believing Lady Hope, but under the circumstances it was quite natural that you should have done so."

Around the same time an acquaintance living in Toronto also wrote to Robertson informing him that they had personal knowledge of Lady Hope and had trusted neither "her judgment or her imagination". He then confided in Robertson that he could "tell a tale" if necessary, and hinted that he knew of some indiscretion he could reveal about her. At the same time this unknown correspondent claimed to have the testimony of one of Darwin's sons (not Francis) who would testify as to the "absolute inaccuracy" of Lady Hope's account. Furthermore, he claimed he had two other (unnamed) sources that would establish that Lady Hope's story was "a fake and a very shameful fake".

This letter which is dated 2 November 1915, only a few weeks after Lady Hope's story appeared, reveals that the writer had been contacted by a Professor Poulton, of Oxford University. Professor Edward Bagnall Poulton, held the Hope chair in zoology at Oxford (which is rather ironic) and was the Richard Dawkins of the day. He was a close friend of Francis Darwin, and was so in awe of Darwin that he considered *On the Origin of Species* to be the greatest of books ever published. The fact that he was behind this attempt to discredit Lady Hope is intriguing, and confirms that there was, at this early stage, an attempt to suffocate the story by blackening Lady Hope's character.

However, despite these attempts by the Darwin family to ruin the reputation of Lady Hope and so stop her story from spreading, the account of Darwin's death-bed conversion took off and soon spread beyond North America and Britain, to India where it appeared in the *Bombay Guardian* of 25 March 1916.

In 1922, Darwin's eldest daughter Henrietta entered the controversy. She had married lawyer Richard Litchfield in 1871 and had settled in London, so was not around Down House when Lady Hope visited Darwin. Nevertheless this did not prevent her denying Lady Hope's story. She had contacted the editor of the influential journal, *The Christian,* and persuaded him to publish a firm denial of the story. This appeared in the issue of 23 February 1922 under the headline, 'Charles Darwin's Death-Bed, Story of Conversion Denied'. The editor explained that from, 'reliable information' the story of Darwin's conversion was 'altogether a fabrication' and that the contradiction was 'from the pen of the eldest daughter of Charles Darwin, Mrs. R.B. Litchfield'. This is what she wrote:

"I was present at his death-bed. Lady Hope was not present during his last illness, or any illness. I believe he never even saw her, but in any case she had no influence over him in any department of thought or belief. He never recanted any of his scientific views, either then or earlier. We think the story of his conversion was fabricated in USA. In most of the versions hymn-singing comes in, and a summer-house where the servants and villagers sang hymns to him. There is no summer-house and no servants or villagers ever sang hymns to him."

The editor added that although he would rejoice to learn that Darwin had been converted, "if there is no evidence that such was the case, it is well that the facts should be known".

Although seriously provoked, Henrietta, had allowed herself to be carried away by her indignation, for she was wrong about the existence of the summer-house. A summer-house did exist in exactly the place Lady Hope's story indicated. It was situated at the far end of the Sandwalk, the place where Darwin would take his daily exercise, and is described in detail by Darwin's granddaughter, Gwen Raverat.[14] She in fact described the chalk drawings still visible on the walls in the 1950s when she wrote her memoir, that had been made by her uncle George and uncle Francis when they had been boys. Furthermore, Henrietta herself has been quoted having recalled the children's nurse, Jessie Brodie sitting in the summer-house at the end of the Sandwalk and being able to hear the 'click-click' of her knitting needles.[15] One wonders how Henrietta had managed to

[14] Gwen Raverat, *Period Place*, p.157
[15] Randal Keynes, *Creation*, p.74

forget about this building which plays such an important part in Lady Hope's story.

Just two weeks after the publication of Henrietta's denial there appeared another letter in, *The Christian*, that further cast doubts as to Mrs. Litchfield's claims.[16] It was from Commissioner Frederick Booth-Tucker of the Salvation Army. Booth-Tucker reported that he had met Lady Hope just a few weeks previously while he was in San Francisco and that she had confirmed the story to him. Booth-Tucker had been a regional judge in the Indian Civil Service before he joined the Salvation Army. He was a brilliant linguist, fluent in Sanskrit, Hindi and Urdu. He had joined the Salvation Army in 1881, and the following year had led a group of Salvationist pioneers to India. William Booth promoted him to be Foreign Secretary of the Salvation Army, and later he acted as Travelling Commissioner. It was in this role that he met Lady Hope in San Francisco where he had travelled to open a new headquarters.

Booth-Tucker had known Lady Hope from his time in London and they had much in common, particularly their Anglo-Indian background. It is likely that their meeting would have been frank and cordial. This is how he recalled it:

[16] F. B. Booth-Tucker, *The Christian*, 9 March 1922

"Lady Hope was conducting meetings in the village shortly before Mr. Darwin's death. She visited him in his home, and he said that he was very pleased to hear about her meetings. She expressed surprise, seeing that she understood that he held contrary views. He replied that a great deal more had been made of some of his views than he had ever intended, and that there was nothing like the Gospel – or words to that effect. Turning to the Bible, which was open before him, he referred to the wonderful depth and beauty of the Epistle to the Hebrews from which he was then reading."

Henrietta was now completely challenged by first hand testimony and responded to Booth-Tucker in a letter dated 23 March 1922 stating:

"It is impossible to know that she [Lady Hope] would say to my belief that Charles Darwin never had any interview with her, Sir Francis Darwin, says that he is certain she never came to Down. I have no doubt that you reported faithfully what Lady Hope told you..."

It is somewhat ironic that just a few days before, on March 14, 1922, in the Court Circular Column of *The Times* there was an announcement of the death of Elizabeth Lady Hope, at Sydney, New South Wales on 8 March.

Both Darwin and Lady Hope were now dead, but there was at this time a growing body of individuals who were very concerned to maintain the war between science and religion. In their eyes this 'war' had only just begun. These individuals did know about the Lady Hope story and were determined to stamp it out. One such person was Henshaw Ward, a close friend of Leonard Darwin. His biography of Darwin had as its title, *Charles Darwin –The Man and his Warfare*, a title that made clear its purpose. Indeed, Henshaw Ward took his vivid prose to great lengths to paint a picture of Darwin's 'War' against Christianity, and reached a climax when it came to the retelling of the notorious Oxford debate of 1860. This he portrayed as a 'furious battle' in which, 'the wildcat in Huxley had been roused...' It had been, 'a fight to the death', in which Huxley had won, when he had 'slain' Bishop Wilberforce. Unfortunately, the resulting impact of this final image was somewhat diminished when he found it necessary to use a biblical metaphor when he declared that, 'the stone had hit the forehead of Goliath'.

However, it was almost another decade before the Lady Hope story was brought to the attention of the public again, this time by Henshaw Ward's friend, Leonard Darwin, the last surviving of Charles and Emma Darwin's children. In a letter to *The Times* on 15 August 1934 he wrote:

"As I grow older my faith in the veracity of mankind gets steadily less and less and now in my eighty-fifth year it is small indeed....a certain lady sent to the Press a long and purely fictitious account of the scene at his [Darwin's] death-bed."

Leonard Darwin was the most controversial of Darwin's children. He had embarked on a military career, but resigned his commission on 'imagined' health grounds. He was elected a member of parliament for three years, but without any notable achievement. In 1907 he was made the first president of the Eugenics Society, and led a campaign for racist advancement. This was to be achieved by selective breeding by encouraging wealthy people to have large families, and to stop poor people having children. Leonard Darwin, and his brother Francis, were both fanatical advocates of racist doctrines, which they believed were an inevitable consequence of their father's theory of evolution as described in *The Origin of Species*. They were therefore determined to protect Darwin's reputation.

In this task they had plenty of support. In the 1880s and subsequent years, an important source of encouragement was the publisher, C.A. Watts. He had established the Rationalist

Press Association, the purpose of which was to produce cheap, and authoritative literature for the mass market, promoting Darwinism, atheism and social humanism. A leading figure in this organisation was Sir Arthur Keith (1866-1955) who held the position of Hunterian Professor at the Royal College of Surgeons. He was also president of the British Association for the Advancement of Science, and in his presidential address at Leeds in 1927, he continued to promote the warfare theme declaring that Darwin had achieved the 'victory'. The humanists had nothing to fear as they had Darwin as their 'consummate General', and that Darwin had spent some twenty years, 'stocking his arsenal'. Darwin's home at Down House was to be preserved as a monument to the great man, it was to become the 'Nazareth of Evolution', a national shrine, and a place of pilgrimage. Furthermore, Darwin had 'launched his campaign at the right moment in time'. The unbelievers had 'won territory' and had 'consolidated their position'. They had now moved on to capture the final 'citadel', namely understanding man's origins, and this had now been achieved, indeed it was one of the 'marvels of the nineteenth century'. This was, in fact, a very apt conclusion for him to reach, as it has subsequently been found that Sir Arthur Keith, the distinguished Hunterian Professor of the Royal College of Surgeons, was no other than the prime suspect for the Piltdown forgery.

For many years these debates rumbled on with freethinkers, humanists and atheists spreading the message that Darwinism had effectively destroyed Christianity, however, with the rise of Hitler and the world once again plunged into war, the majority of people had other concerns. It was not until after the Second World War that further interest was taken in the Lady Hope story. In the monthly journal, *A Message from God*, published in October 1955, the account was again reprinted, and then in February 1957 it was repeated in the *Monthly Record of the Free Church of Scotland*. These articles created considerable interest, as well as comment in the correspondence section of *The Scotsman*. This prompted Nora Barlow (Charles Darwin's granddaughter, and youngest child of Horace Darwin) to respond. In a letter to *The Scotsman* published on, Thursday 8 May, 1958 she wrote: "The correspondence that has arisen in *The Scotsman* over Charles Darwin's alleged visit by Lady Hope is perpetuating a myth that was authoritatively denied in 1922 by those in the best position to judge of its truth or falsity." Nora Barlow had edited and revised numerous manuscripts of her grandfather, including his autobiography, and had published those sections that had originally been deleted in earlier editions, particularly some of Darwin's comments on religion. In her letter to *The Scotsman* she paraphrases much of the contents of her aunt Henrietta's earlier letter to *The Christian*, but adds nothing new.

This was the last time a member of the Darwin family published a denunciation of Lady Hope's story. It was now left to others to defend their protestations. However, the most damning discovery was not published in any religious journal, but in the pages of the atheistic magazine, *The Humanist*. In 1960, and then in 1965, two articles were published, not from the pen of a Christian defending the reputation of Lady Hope, but from a prominent unbeliever. The author was Pat Sloan. Patrick Alan Sloan had been born in 1908 and educated at Cambridge University, where he had had a distinguished academic career. He had then worked in the Soviet Union from 1931 to 1937, teaching at a Soviet college. He returned to England and following the Second World War he became a leading pro-Soviet propagandist, becoming General Secretary of the British Soviet friendship Society. The commentator, Bernard Levin once called him an "old party bonehead".[17] Bonehead, or not, he did have concerns about the treatment of Christians in the Soviet Union and was a frequent correspondent to *The Times* on this matter. This probably endeared him to the Very Reverend Hewlett Johnson, the so-called "Red Dean" of

---

[17] Bernard Levin, *The Times*, 23 March 1972.

Canterbury, who counted him to be a friend. On one occasion the "Red Dean" told how his friend had been taken ill while in the Soviet Union and during a stay in a Russian hospital he had been nursed by an evangelical Christian who had tried to convert him. Although he hadn't been converted, the kindness he had received so affected him that he was sympathetic towards Christianity. It is possibly on this account that he became intrigued by the Darwin conversion story and he began to investigate it.

The result was the two articles that were published in *The Humanist*. Although Sloan had not been able to identify Lady Hope, he had however concluded that, despite the Darwin family's claims, it was likely that a lady evangelist had visited Darwin towards the end of his life, possibly a collaborator of James Fegan, and who possibly had become a 'Lady Hope' by marriage subsequently. These findings gave credibility to the alleged encounter as published in 1915. This was a devastating outcome for the Darwin family, however, for some mysterious reason, Sloan's detective work remained unrecognised for many years, although it was referred to by Sir Hedley Atkins in his book, *Down : The Home of the Darwins*, published in 1974.

In his book, Atkins puts the record straight as to the existence of the summer-house. "There was a summer-house at the end of the Sandwalk", he concluded, so confirming that Henrietta Darwin had been wrong in her protestations. However, he could throw no light as to the identity of Lady Hope, referring to her as "a somewhat shadowy figure".

A decade later, the distinguished biographer, Ronald Clark, published his biography, *The Survival of Charles Darwin*, in which he claimed that the deathbed legend had been "manufactured". And although he correctly identifies Lady Hope as the widow of Admiral of the Fleet, Sir James Hope, he gets his facts wrong when he stated that Lady Hope's account had been given 'shortly after Darwin's death' when in fact it was some thirty years afterwards, and when he claimed that it had been published in 1915, with Dwight Moody's encouragement, when in fact Moody had been dead some sixteen years.

In the centenary year of Darwin's death in April 1982, Irvine Stone in an article in the *New Scientist* entitled 'The Death of Darwin,' reiterated the consensus at the time and stated:

"Upon word of his [Darwin's] death, his detractors circulated a rumour that he had repented on his deathbed, and asked God's forgiveness for his blasphemies. There was not an iota of truth in the charge, yet it still surfaces today..."

It was shortly afterwards that I began to investigate the story and was able to quickly identify Lady Hope. I was, however, mystified as to how previous investigators had not been able to identify her. Sloan had referred to her as, "the elusive Lady Hope", and Atkins described her as, "a somewhat shadowy figure..." I found that her identity could easily be found in any public library, as she was listed in the *Catalogue of the British Library*, as being the author of some thirty-seven books, including a detailed biography of her father, General Sir Arthur Cotton. I was completely puzzled as to why successive writers had perpetuated her existence as a myth.

I thought that clarifying the identity of Lady Hope and establishing that she had been a real person and not a myth was of some interest to the scientific community. Accordingly, I wrote a short article on my findings and on, April 21, 1988, I submitted it to the journal *Nature*, for publication in the correspondence section. A few weeks later, I received a rebuff from the editor, stating that the article was being returned as it did not have a compelling claim on the journal's space. The upshot was that I decided to publish my findings in the book,

The Life and Death of Charles Darwin, which was published the following year.

Although, as any author, I had expected some criticism and adverse comment, I was unprepared for the scathing and vicious personal attacks that followed. This being so, it has been of some satisfaction to see how the *New Scientist* has had to eat its own words. In a review of the book published on, May 13, 1989 it wrote with respect to Lady Hope's account:

"The evidence for this pious scene is the testimony of the water-drinking evangelist, whom Darwin's daughter denied he ever knew. Croft concludes confidently it is accurate. This is no joke Croft is not the kind of author who makes jokes."

But some twenty years later, the *New Scientist* was not so confident, "the original story cannot be dismissed as pure invention" it wrote quoting Professor James Moore of the Open University.[18]

Moore, a biographer of Darwin had entered the debate on publication of his book, *The Darwin Legend*, in 1995. In this book he confirmed much of what I had uncovered about Lady Hope, however, he concluded that although she almost certainly

[18] Amanda Gefter, review of the book, *Galileo Goes to Jail*, *New Scientist*, 2009

had visited Darwin, possibly on several occasions, when she related her story some thirty years after the meeting, she had exaggerated facts, or alternatively had imagined things, or fabricated the occasion in order to impress people. It was all self-aggrandizement, declared Moore. The woman had been disgraced in Britain by bankruptcy, "*The Times* had carried the humiliating story," he wrote and she had, "retreated to New York City....with little but a second-hand title to her name."

Thus instead of establishing facts, Moore used character assassination, to discredit Lady Hope. The only evidence he could uncover were some "reconstructed" letters, that had been put together by a colleague from carbon copies of two of James Fegan's letters, which he had written to individuals inquiring as to Lady Hope's story. And it was on the basis of this incomplete documentation that he had built his case. In one of the letters Fegan is reputed to have written:

"When she [Lady Hope] was leaving here for America she asked me to give her a commendatory letter to use in America and I had the painful duty of telling her I could not do so."[19]

In a later chapter the credibility of this evidence will be brought into question, when it will be shown to be unreliable, a

---

[19] James Moore, *The Darwin Legend*, p. 110

fact that might also have occurred to Moore himself, as in his subsequent writing on this subject, he fails to place any reliance on it.[20]

So much for the background to Lady Hope's story, which is now referred to as "a myth", "a legend", and "a fabrication". Lady Hope herself is said to be, "a shadowy figure", "an illusion" and "an hallucination" so to progress we must look at the woman herself and to look at what is known about her. This will be done in the following chapters.

---

[20] James Moore, *Galileo Goes to Jail*, pp. 142-151

Chapter 6

Miss Cotton

Lady Hope was born Elizabeth Reid Cotton on, December 9, 1842 in Hobart Town, Tasmania, the first child of Arthur Thomas Cotton (1803-99) and his wife Elizabeth (née Learmouth, 1814-1907). At the time her father was a captain with the Royal Engineers and was in the colony on sick leave, as a result of exhaustion following prolonged work on the construction of anicuts (dams) across the Cauvery and Coleroon rivers in the Madras Presidency of Southern India (now the modern state of Tamil Nadu). He belonged to an aristocratic military family that could trace their roots back as far as the twelfth century to the Abbey of Combermere in Cheshire. His cousin was General Sir Stapleton Cotton who at the time of Elizabeth's birth was the Viscount Combermere. Elizabeth's mother was born Elizabeth Livingstone Learmouth on, June 1, 1814 at Polmont, near Stirling, the daughter of Thomas Learmouth (1783-1869) and Christian Donald. She had moved to Tasmania with her father who had established himself as a successful merchant in Hobart Town. He later became a large land owner in Australia and had business interests in wool production in Geelong, Australia, as well as in India. The family were strict Presbyterians.

Captain Arthur Cotton and Miss Elizabeth Learmouth married on, October 29, 1841, in Hobart Town, and following the birth of their first child, Elizabeth, they returned to India and settled in the town of Vizagapatam in Madras. Captain Cotton then became involved in his major work involving the construction of irrigation schemes in the Godavari Delta. The Godavari region was in a desperate condition on account of recent famines when millions of people had perished on account of starvation. Arthur Cotton's ambitious plan was to build huge dams across the Godavari River. The project started in 1847 and took five years to complete. It was a massive undertaking as the width of the river was some four miles, however it was a most successful scheme that resulted in saving many millions of lives. Indeed the people of this part of India still revere Arthur Cotton and consider him a major hero, so much so, that he is the only Englishman who has had monuments put up to his memory since Independence. Both Captain Cotton, and his wife were deeply religious, and young Elizabeth was brought up to have a strong Christian faith. When she was about eight years old, once a week, she would travel alone on horseback, "...over a very steep pass and through the hills..." to a distant mission station, "a lovely cottage all covered in jessamine and roses" where she would have Bible reading with a missionary. Many years later she recalled that : "Some of the things which he taught me I shall never forget..."[21] Around 1854, when she was entering her teenage years the family returned to England. They set sail from Madras on March 8, for a voyage of four months. During this voyage, there was an outbreak of smallpox on board and some fourteen passengers died. It was a melancholic time and they were grateful when they eventually arrived at Gravesend on July, 2, later she recalled her feelings: "How pleasant it was to find ourselves on firm ground and in the England I had heard and read so much about."[22]

On their arrival in England they stayed with their friend the Reverend Frederick Chalmers at the Beckenham Rectory and then for a time settled in Tunbridge Wells. Her father who was now Colonel Cotton was in poor health after many years in tropical climates, so for a time they moved to Weston-super-Mare and, then the following spring, to the Cotswolds. In 1856 they were on the move again and settled in London but they found the air pollution affected them and the whole family went down with whooping cough. Sadly, Elizabeth's younger sister died, she later recalled : "My father was very ill, and my little

[21] Lady Hope, *Sunny Footsteps, or when I was a child*, p.83
[22] Ibid., p.121

sister, to our great grief, succumbed to it leaving a blank that has never been filled."[23]

Towards the end of 1856 they rented a house in Hadley Green on the outskirts of Barnet. This proved a healthy place to live, yet was within easy reach of London. Shortly afterwards the missionary David Livingstone also settled in the area and he became a family friend. They also made friends with Mr. Wilbraham Taylor, whose daughter, Janetta Mary, was the same age as young Elizabeth and they became close friends. She was also a devout Christian and later became a noted hymn writer.[24] The family worshipped at Christ Church where the vicar was the Reverend William Pennefather (1816-73). Pennefather and his wife Catherine were to have a great influence on the family. They were both evangelicals, and around this time, Pennefather started the annual Mildmay Conference, at which in years to come Elizabeth was to become a well-respected speaker.

Shortly after the family settled in Hadley Green, Colonel Cotton was required to return to India, this being around the time of the Indian Mutiny, so consequently it was a very tense period for the family. This was made worse by the death of her brother Arthur Stokes from whooping cough on May, 11, 1859

---

[23] Lady Hope, *General Sir Arthur Cotton, His Life and Work*, p. 172
[24] Janetta Mary Wilbraham Taylor Trench (1843-1925)

when he was just seven years of age. Thus within the space of a year young Elizabeth had lost both a sister and a brother, thus making her father's absence in India more keenly felt.

In India, Colonel Cotton had been appointed Commandant of Engineers in the Madras Presidency and advised on all irrigation projects throughout the whole of sub-continent. On his return to England in 1860, his achievements were recognised when he was awarded a knighthood from Queen Victoria. Then on Wednesday February 20, 1861, a public banquet was held in London, in his honour. Lord Shaftesbury was in the chair with some two hundred other distinguished persons present. The following day *The Morning Chronicle* reported the event and spoke of the "brilliant achievements" Colonel Cotton had done in improving the condition of the people of India.

The following year he left his family again and returned to India to supervise the Behar irrigation project in the Sone river valley. Meanwhile his family were once again on the move and settled in Tunbridge Wells to await his return.

On his return to England he was asked by the government to investigate the Bradfield Reservoir disaster in Sheffield that had occurred on the night of Friday March, 11, 1864, when the reservoir some 8 miles from Sheffield burst its bank, and the water swept everything away in its path, with the loss of hundreds of lives.

Following this period in Sheffield the family then travelled to County Down in Ireland at the invitation of the Earl of Roden (Robert Jocelyn, 1788-1870). Robert Jocelyn, the third earl, had married Maria Stapleton who was a relative of Colonel Cotton. Both the earl and his wife were evangelicals and their home at Tollymore Park, near Newcastle in Co. Down had become a haven for evangelicals. At this date, Colonel Cotton who had served some forty years in tropical India, was completely exhausted, so their invitation to Tollymore was welcomed.

They were to stay in Ireland for some three years when they rented a beautiful property, with gardens, stables and orchard, known locally as The Nest, in the village of Bryansford.[25] It was at Tollymore that young Elizabeth met many of the leading evangelicals of the day who were associated with Lord Roden. There was Sir Arthur Blackwood, for many years Head of the Post Office, and president of the Mildmay Conference, and another visitor was Miss Catherine Marsh. Catherine Marsh was widely known as the author of *Memorials*

---

[25] It is still there today and is a picturesque rambling property, it is a listed building that until recently was a study centre.

of Captain Hedley Vicars, published in 1855, being an account of the life and death of a Christian soldier in the Crimean War, which had become a bestseller. Miss Marsh had done much to help the sick and dying during the cholera epidemic of 1866, and subsequently opened a hospital in Brighton for the poor. Meeting these devout Christians was an inspiration to young Elizabeth and gave her the determination to devote her life to helping others.

In May 1866 her father was promoted to Major General and received the Star of India award and was made a Knight Commander. His health had, by this time, improved sufficiently for him to return to public life. In the June the following year he gave lectures to the Royal Geographical Society, and in September, to the British Association meeting in Dundee. On many of these occasions young Elizabeth accompanied him as his assistant, which gave her the opportunity to meet many of the leading scientists of the day.

In 1869 they decided to settle in the town of Dorking in Surrey. At this time, Dorking had a population of about 5,400, and was undergoing a period of substantial growth. It was while living in Dorking that young Elizabeth began her evangelistic and philanthropic work that was to occupy her for the rest of her life. It had started in a very small way with a Sunday School class, but from this beginning her mission took off. At this time, it was not felt right for women to preach, and even women like Catherine Booth had had difficulty in becoming accepted, however, young Elizabeth had the support and encouragement of her father. Only a few years before the American evangelist, Mrs. Phoebe Palmer, had visited Britain and caused outrage amongst male clergy who had objected to her preaching. To much of the public at this time the possibility of female ministry was scandalous. In particular, it would have been highly presumptuous for a twenty-something girl to be seen preaching the Gospel to men. However, unlike what had happened with Catherine Booth, young Elizabeth had no struggle with the problem of a woman's rights to a Christian ministry, she simply by-passed it.

She had started with a Sunday school class for girls, and she went on from this to have a boys class, 'wild boys who thronged the streets on Sunday afternoons, uncared for and untaught.' The class proved so successful that her father rented a larger room to accommodate the numbers, and then working men wanted to attend. And so a men's meeting was started and from this developed the idea of a 'Coffee Room' where working men could obtain non-alcoholic drinks and food, and where she could hold Bible classes and prayer meetings. Over the months it expanded to two rooms, one a coffee room and the other a meeting room. She had the walls decorated with maps and religious pictures, it was always kept warm with food and drink always available. There were places for people to sit down and tables on which they could write letters or occupy themselves. Many years later, in 1960, William Dinnage, a local boy, published his memoirs of Old Dorking and recalled being taken to the Coffee Room by his father he wrote:

"I well remember on several occasions being taken there by my father and noticing the few coloured prints on the walls, 'The Good Shepherd' and other similar scenes from the gospels.'[26]

And, "Miss Cotton also conducted a Sunday evening service at 8 o'clock in the large upper room at the public hall...a good number of the congregation were non-church-goers. These services drew large audiences and Miss Cotton became popular. She had a pleasing, engaging manner and silvery voice, and her message was simple..."

It is clear she believed in an active form of Christianity, and although she felt that the Church of England had failed in its mission to reach many of the working class, she nevertheless remained an Anglican, and believed that her mission extended

---

[26] William Henry Dinnage, (1870-1963) *Dinnages' Recollections of Old Dorking*, p.4-5

beyond sectarian boundaries by introducing a simple form of worship for working people.

Over the following years the Coffee Room project was enlarged to include a 'penny bank' where men could save their money instead of spending it on beer, a shoe club and an outdoor coffee stall. On Whit Monday she took a party of men on a holiday to the sea-side at Eastbourne. She recalled that many of them had never seen the sea before and that afterwards many of them "often alluded to this delightful Whit Monday, saying it was one of the happiest times they ever spent in their lives."[27]

In 1876, Elizabeth published an account of her work in the book, *Our Coffee Room*. This book was warmly received and it went into many editions. Florence Nightingale was greatly impressed by it and commended it in a letter published in *The Times* of, March 27, 1878, and she is known to have given an inscribed copy to one of the soldiers she had nursed back to health during the Crimean War.[28]

In *Our Coffee Room*, Elizabeth comes across as a woman of incredible charisma and charm, as well as revealing herself to

---

[27] Elizabeth Cotton, *Our Coffee Room*, p.145
[28] There exists a copy of the second edition inscribed by Florence Nightingale on July 18, 1876, to Robert Robinson, drummer boy of the 68th Light Infantry during the Crimean War.

have an intriguing sense of humour. It is clear that her charisma was derived from her great love for others, particularly those who had no-one to care for them.

However, her work was not done without considerable opposition. Firstly, there were those clergy who opposed a woman preacher. She recalled the afternoon when a clergyman came with a large party of interested persons to inspect the Coffee Room. He was shown all the work that was going on including the prayer room, where daily prayer meetings took place. As he sat down to take a cup of tea after his tour of inspection, he smilingly said, 'I approve of all the secular part of the work,' but he disapproved of the prayer and Bible-reading, presumably on account of her being a woman.

However, she knew she had the support of all the working men, and she was confident the Bible was on her side, indeed she had a compendious knowledge of the Bible, and even in her twenties, she was an expert on the text, and could argue on equal terms with most clergy.

But opposition was not just from the clergy. Many of her social circle were opposed to her work. After dinner one evening she was attacked by guests who considered her temperance work was not beneficial to working men. 'A coffee-room without beer,' they said in one voice, 'would you deprive the poor man of his beer? His little comfort, his one pleasure!'[29]

However, she was not discouraged. She was convinced that total abstinence was necessary in order to remove much of the misery in society. But this, at the time, was not a popular message. In fact it was a dangerous message for a young woman to promote. One only has to think of how the Salvation Army was attacked in its early days, and closer to home, her friend Lady Ailsa, also a temperance campaigner, had received death threats. Elizabeth, however, was an indomitable woman who had no fear. She was convinced that she was in God's service, and was not intimidated by the hooligans that might be bribed by the brewers and publicans to attack her, or, her work. Indeed, she represented herself perfectly in the story of, 'The Burglar', when the lady was attacked by a desperate man armed with a pistol. "If you scream I'll blow your brains out," he said, when she calmly replied,"Well, I'm not the sort of woman to scream."[30]

On one occasion when Bible reading at the Dorking Cottage Hospital she was warned about one of the patients, "a terrible character...a very turbulent and disagreeable man who

[29] Elizabeth Cotton, *More About our Coffee Room*, p.122
[30] Lady Hope, *His Handiwork*, p.21

drank hard and was a great fighter." Instead of avoiding him she walked over to him, touched his hand, and told him about the love of Jesus. Sometime later, she was again at the hospital when he was discharged, and he offered to walk her home up Tower Hill. On reaching her house, he turned to her and announced, "I want to give my heart to Jesus. When shall I do it?"

"When!" she replied. "Tonight, to be sure...Now is the accepted time; now is the day of salvation."

"I should like you to pray with me," he said very earnestly.

So she took him into the house, to her sitting room, and they knelt down together and prayed. Decorum did not require evangelicals to have a chaperon.

One instance that illustrates Elizabeth's involvement with the working men is the case of the young railway guard whom she brought to Christ, but who subsequently fell ill with a serious illness (presumably tuberculosis) and eventually died. The man's colleagues from the railway company, attended the Coffee Room following the funeral for refreshments and a short memorial service, but Elizabeth was so full of emotion she had great difficulty in speaking.[31]

As a consequence Elizabeth was greatly admired and genuinely loved by those she encountered. Some indication of this may be gained from their response to her. On one occasion a group of workmen from a building firm in London had been given a day's holiday, when they had gone on a ramble over Box Hill, and then turned up at the Coffee Room for supper, not realising that it was also a mission hall. Elizabeth was there and after handing out some tracts, she offered a prayer for God's blessing on them and their homes. She recalled that the men gave, "a general look of amazement". She then over-heard one man whisper to his mate, "but this is hardly the time for it." She then tackled the man and a discussion ensued as to whether religion could be for both rich and poor. It concluded when all the men had come to her opinion, when she suggested they sing some hymns. Afterwards, the man who had spoken out came to her and apologised, she recalled, "we parted the warmest of friends, he accepting a small Bible with maps from me before he left." But that was not the end of the incident. A week afterwards, she received a letter from the head of the building firm, "saying that his men had all requested him to express to

---

[31] Elizabeth Cotton, *More About Our Coffee Room*, p.154

her 'their grateful thanks for the interest' she had taken in them on their visit to Dorking, and that they had enjoyed a very pleasant day..."[32]

To show their appreciation she received many gifts from the working men she helped. On one occasion 160 railway men of the London-Brighton line at Dorking presented her with a pair of solid silver candlesticks together with an illuminated testimonial signed by them all, in gratitude for her religious services.[33] In her book, *Lines of Light on a Dark Background*, she recalled that her drawing room was garnished with the many gifts she had received from loving and grateful people, albeit she apologised for having entered into the details. But probably, the most revealing, was the present she received early on the Christmas morning of 1874, and it was some five years later she recorded the extraordinary event:

"Some of the men paid us a midnight visit at Christmas about five years ago. Having a hint that some of the men from the night-school were coming up to bring me a present I looked out of one of the windows overhanging our garden, and saw a light steadily moving up the path that crossed the field to our house. Soon the mysterious glimmer halted and we could see some of

---

[32] Elizabeth Cotton, *More about Our Coffee Room*, p.229-231
[33] cf. *Birmingham Daily Post*, Thursday 21 March, 1878

the dusky figures surrounding it. On going out to greet the group of nocturnal visitors I was told by them that they had come to put up a pedestal carved and made entirely by one of themselves and surmounted by a large vase intended for holding flowering and creeping plants...It was not until morning that we saw the immense labour and perseverance they had displayed in the accomplishment of this presentation; the reason for its arrival at that late hour being that a Christmas morning surprise was intended."[34]

[34] Lady Hope, *Lines of Light on a Dark Background*, p.138

Chapter 7

Lady Hope

During the summer of 1874 Elizabeth Cotton assisted in the revival mission of the American evangelists, Moody and Sankey. The highlight of the mission had been Dwight Moody preaching to some 20,000 people on the slopes of Arthur's Seat in Edinburgh. Elizabeth was one of his important helpers in counselling many of the women who had turned to Christ, and she continued with this work as the mission went to other major centres throughout Scotland. In all she spent six weeks in Scotland, and in late August sailed down the Caledonian Canal, to hold the concluding meetings in Campbeltown, after which she joined Moody and his party at Balinakill House, the home of Sir William McKinnon. McKinnon had made his fortune in his shipping company, the British India Steamship Company (later to become P & O). He was an evangelical who supported the Moody revival; he also supported H.M.Stanley's expeditions to Africa.

During the spring and summer of the following year Elizabeth helped with Moody's London campaign. By this time she was herself an established evangelist. She was now addressing large audiences throughout the country and sharing the platform with such eminent people as Baroness Burdett-Coutts, and Lord Cairns. The Earl of Shaftesbury writing in the Preface to her second book, *More About Our Coffee Room*, described her as : "The pious, amiable and accomplished young lady whose efforts are therein recorded, has given an example of what may be done by the exertions, though but of one person, founded on an intense love of the gospel, and a burning desire to convey it to the souls of others. Everyone who reads her achievements cannot but rejoice in the harvest she has reaped..."[35]

On December 6, 1877, she married Admiral Sir James Hope at St Paul's Church in Dorking, and they moved to his family estate at Carriden on the Firth of Forth. Elizabeth was marrying into a very distinguished naval family. The bridegroom was the son of Admiral Sir George Hope who had commanded the battleship, HMS *Defence* at Trafalgar. He also had had a equally distinguished military record. He had followed his father and had served in the Crimean War in command of HMS *Majestic*. Then in 1859, he had been made commander-in-chief in China, during the Second Opium War.

---

[35] Elizabeth Cotton, *More about Our Coffee Room*, Preface

He had been involved in the capture of Peking and had been severely wounded on two occasions. He was appointed Admiral in 1870, and in 1873 had been made the principal naval aide-de-camp to Queen Victoria.

Admiral Hope (1808-1881) was a devout Christian and temperance advocate. He had established at Carriden a model village for the estate workers, known as Muirhouses, consisting of about a dozen houses, a schoolhouse and a library (today it is a conservation area of historic interest). Carriden was close to the sea-side port of Bo'ness, which had been at one time a major whaling port, but now the main industries were coal mining and iron smelting. On arrival in the area Elizabeth found that drunkenness was a major problem so she started a coffee room as she had done at Dorking, and this proved extremely successful. Admiral Hope supported his wife in her work and accompanied her around the country as she spread the message of the gospel and of temperance. Now Lady Hope of Carriden she began to attract large crowds, as she did when she addressed three separate meetings at Lancaster on the weekend of November 15, 1878, when it was reported that she was "most heartily received" by crowded audiences. She began to spread the temperance message and a Coffee Room was opened at Maybole by her friend the Marchioness of Ailsa of Culzean

Castle. On these occasions the Admiral joined her on the platform giving his encouragement, however, his health was not good and in the autumn of 1880 he was not able to continue this support. His health deteriorated rapidly and he died at Carriden House on, June 9, 1881, age 73 years. Elizabeth was now a widow.

Following her husband's death she remained for a short period with her parents in Dorking, then, after settling her affairs in Scotland, she resumed her temperance and gospel evangelism. It was sometime this autumn that she visited Charles Darwin at Down House, probably while she was staying with the evangelist James Fegan's mother, who lived in Darwin's village. From notes in Emma Darwin's diary for 1881, it is known that she visited Mrs. Fegan that year on, 7th November. On Emma Darwin's return to Down House she would have told Darwin of Lady Hope's presence in the village. The upshot being that Darwin sent Lady Hope an invitation to visit him. It is possible that the Darwins had already been introduced to her as they had visited Dorking on numerous occasions to stay with their relatives at Abinger Hall just outside Dorking. Indeed, Darwin had visited Dorking almost every summer from 1873 to 1880. This was the period when Elizabeth Cotton (as she was then) was making news with her temperance work in the area. Besides, it is almost certain that Darwin would have been familiar with her father, General Sir Arthur Cotton, not only on account of his remarkable work in India, but on account of his horticultural claims following his use of the "deep cultivation" system of growing crops. Darwin would have known about this from the many reports in the press that had recorded remarkable yields of crops obtained with this system. It is also possible that Darwin had heard of Lady Hope and her father from his relative Mr. Thomas Farrer, of Abinger Hall, who was himself a keen horticulturist.

In the months following their encounter Lady Hope lived for a while in Bournemouth, possibly staying at the home of the former Lord Chancellor, Lord Cairns, who made his residence, known as 'Lindisfarne' available as a retreat for evangelists. It was while she was there that she opened several new coffee rooms in the area, as well as on the Isle of Wight, and shared a platform at a temperance conference with Darwin's former *Beagle* colleague, Admiral Sir Bartholomew Sulivan.

On leaving Bournemouth she was engaged, with Professor Henry Drummond, in planning and organising, Moody's second mission to Britain during the years 1883-84. She then settled in London, where she was involved in the work of the Golden Bells Mission, in Notting Hill Gate, and was actively engaged in taking the gospel message to the poor people in the slums of the city. Much of her experiences at this time she recorded in her book, *Our Golden Key: A Narrative of Facts from Outcast London.* This is a unique record of the conditions of the poor at the time, when they were all crowded together in courts and 'rookeries'. In one chapter she describes the conditions she found :

"Children were sleeping in cupboards, on shelves, one above another, some of them almost naked, all ill-clothed and unclean. But, indeed, if we were to examine the fashions of this strangely – misnamed court, we should discover without much difficulty that they consisted chiefly of rags and tatters and ill-concealed nakedness."[36]

And on another occasion,

"At the further end of the court two wretched half-clothed women were fighting desperately, striving to tear one another to pieces in their rage and fury. It was a sickening sight. Their hair was wild and unkempt; their clothes ragged; their voices shrieks from evil depths, reminding one of the words applied to the unhallowed tongue, 'set on fire of hell'"

---

[36] Lady Hope, *Our Golden Key – A narrative of facts from Outcast London,,* p. 12

She then concentrated her effort at providing decent accommodation for working men, and at one stage was providing some thousand beds a night, to the homeless in the city.

In September 1893, she married the widower, Mr. T. A. Denny, whom she had known for many years. Denny was a very wealthy and shrewd businessman, who had made his fortune in the meat trade. Like Lady Hope, he was an evangelical, and also had been involved in the Moody and Sankey missions. He was also a major supporter of the Salvation Army, and had helped William Booth purchase the Army's headquarters as well as their new printing press. Following their marriage, Lady Hope and Mr. Denny worked together, opening new large hostels for working men, and providing decent accommodation, at a reasonable cost. In this work they were extremely successful and at the time of the War in the Transvaal, they were providing much needed accommodation for the returning soldiers, many of whom were severely wounded.

Lady Hope then began what was to be her most ambitious project. It was the Connaught Club for working men. It was a hugely expensive project and was aimed at providing accommodation for male servants, and other homeless men, in the capital. It was a grand project, and was meant to be self-supporting, for there was a restaurant, and some seven shops on the ground floor. She was now providing much needed accommodation to several thousand every night, all in a temperance and Christian environment. Unfortunately her good works attracted much unwanted attention, particularly from those individuals who thought they could exploit her kindness and generosity. While her husband was alive she was largely protected, however following his death in December 1909, she became vulnerable and fell prey to an unscrupulous and ruthless individual. The man went under numerous aliases, but was known to her as Mr. Gerald Fry. He was clearly a very plausible individual and had been well educated and had come from a good family. It is possible she may even have known of his father, who had worked in Madras in India, around the same time as her own father.

Gerald Fry, however, had been disowned by his own family. His career as a rogue would take several volumes to document, for he was probably the most notorious conman of the time. He had been in prison many times, with sentences of hard labour, and he had been accused of the attempted murder of his wife and children. In addition he had been responsible, through his dishonesty, for the bankruptcy of several other people. Lady Hope was almost certainly completely unaware of his background. She had come across him as an alcoholic, in need of a chance, and she had fallen for his hard luck story. She paid for his rehabilitation in a drying-out clinic, and on his discharge, she set him up in a small business. But he could see there was more money, where his help had come from and he talked his way into handling all her finances. Lady Hope at this time was almost seventy years of age and had recently been widowed, so she was clearly very vulnerable. The result was only too predictable. But it was too late when she discovered he had swindled her, and in 1911 she was declared bankrupt.

For a woman of her social standing this must have been devastating. Although, she knew it was none of her fault, the personal disgrace and humiliation were inescapable. However, she still had friends and she was determined to continue with her temperance work and evangelism, but not in Britain. North America was to be her new field of activity, and in 1913 she left England, and settled in New York. Here she became involved and assisted in the Billy Sunday missions. William 'Billy' Sunday had been a popular baseball player in the National League, but following his conversion he became an influential evangelist. She also worked with the Salvation Army.

In 1915, she attended the Moody Northfield Conference where she related her story about her meeting with Charles

Darwin. This was immediately picked up by the newspapers and the story quickly spread around the world. Later she moved to the West Coast and settled in Los Angeles where she made friends with a group of Christians who, following her death, signed an affidavit vouching for her story about Charles Darwin. It was around this time, while on a visit to San Francisco, that she came across an old friend, Commissioner Booth-Tucker who was in California to open a new headquarters for the Salvation Army. Booth-Tucker asked her about the Darwin story and she confirmed the details to him. Booth-Tucker had been a district judge in India, and had a brilliant legal mind. It is possible he told her about the rumours that were circulating in England about her integrity, and about how Francis Darwin had publicly accused her of dishonesty. It is clear that his advice as a lawyer would have been for her to defend her reputation in court. So it is possible that her decision to return to England, at this juncture, was motivated by her desire to clear her name. Unfortunately, she had been diagnosed with breast cancer, and while staying in Sydney Australia, en route home, she was admitted to the Burilda Private Hospital where she died on, March 8, 1922. Her death was announced in the Court Circular column of *The Times* on 14 March, and her last Will, which was proved at the High Court in London, in February the following year, indicated that her estate was £296-5s-6d.

As all libel lawyers will confirm, it is very difficult to predict the outcome of a defamation trial, however the claimant (or plaintiff, as it would have been at this time) did not have to prove anything, it was the defendant that had to prove his case, and Francis Darwin would have had great difficulty convincing a jury that Lady Hope had been dishonest. He had not been at Down house at the time of her visit, and there were no witnesses as to her conversation with Darwin. I believe, that in the event of a trial, Lady Hope would have been completely vindicated.

Chapter 8

The Fegan Letters

If this matter had reached the Courts, then one important witness would have been James William Condell Fegan. J.W.C. Fegan, who had been born in 1852, became a leading figure in the late nineteenth century humanitarian movement, and established residential homes for orphan boys. He was an evangelist and a member of the strict Plymouth Brethren. On account of his parents retiring to Downe village in 1880, he had become acquainted with Darwin. Darwin, in fact, greatly admired this young energetic Christian, who had attracted the support of Lord Shaftesbury in establishing a home for orphan boys at Stony Stratford.

During the August of 1880, Fegan brought a group of these boys to Downe for a camping holiday, and they visited Down House, when they sang hymns on the lawn for Darwin. Darwin had been so impressed as to give each of the boys a sixpence piece.

The following year, Fegan held revivalist meetings in a tent in the village, but when the weather became colder the meetings became impracticable, and he asked Darwin for permission to use a small building, on the edge of his estate, that had been used as a reading room for the villagers. Darwin was only too happy to let him have the use of the building and wrote him the following letter:[37]

"Dear Mr. Fegan,

You ought not to have to write to me for permission to use the reading room. You have far more right to it than we have, for your services have done more for the village in a few months than all our efforts for many years. We have never been able to reclaim a drunkard, but through your services I do not know that there is a drunkard left in the village.

Now may I have the pleasure of handing the reading room over to you? Perhaps, if we should want it some night for a special purpose, you will be good enough to let us use it.

Yours sincerely,

Charles Darwin"

Following the transfer of the reading room to Fegan it became known as the Gospel Room, and later the Gospel Hall, Fegan later recalled:

---

[37] Fullerton, *J.W.C. Fegan, A Tribute*, p.30

"The services I held were attended sometimes by members of the Darwin family, and regularly by members of their household. Indeed when I had a Mission in Downe, the Darwin family were considerate enough to alter their dinner hour so that their household might attend.... At the services, Parslow, the old family butler was converted to God and brought into Church membership, also Mrs. Sales, the housekeeper, was brought into the light and others."[38]

We definitely know that services were held during the February (probably between 14 to 16th) of 1881, for Emma Darwin wrote the following in a letter to her daughter Henrietta:

"Hurrah for Mr. Fegan! Mrs. Evans [the cook] attended a prayer meeting in which old M. made 'as nice a prayer as ever you heard in your life...' ('Old M' being described in a footnote as 'a notable old drunkard in the village).[39]

Thus from these facts it can be seen that the evangelist James Fegan was actively working in Darwin's village at the time Lady Hope met Darwin. In fact, at this time the village of Downe had become a hotbed of revivalism with evangelical gatherings and conversions taking place right at the bottom of Darwin's garden. Indeed, it is likely that Lady Hope was

---

[38] Fullerton, *J.W.C. Fegan A tribute*, p. 31
[39] H. Litchfield (ed) *Emma Darwin – A Century of Family Letter*, vol 2, p.244

staying with Fegan's mother, who, like Lady Hope herself, had recently been widowed. Whether Lady Hope was actually helping with Fegan's mission is not clear. She had probably been conducting tent meetings among the Kent hop pickers in the weeks before and was now, conducting Bible readings in the local villages. As we know that Emma Darwin visited Mrs. Fegan on November 7, it is conceivable that Darwin, on hearing of Lady Hope's presence in the village, sent her an invitation to Down House.

As already mentioned, it is possible that they had already met, or else Darwin had met her father. He would certainly have known about the General's remarkable claims regarding the 'deep cultivation' system he had devised on his land at Dorking. What becomes clear from her account is that he was very pleased to see her, and this is understandable. She was a very charismatic, charming young woman, with few of the puritan prejudices one might expect in a female evangelist. Furthermore, they had in common their advocacy of temperance. Darwin, for most of his life, had held a 'horror' of drunkenness, and had constantly warned his children of the dangers inherent in consuming alcohol. These concerns probably had their origin in the fact that both his grandmother, and great-grandmother had died of alcoholism, and over the years he had become convinced that no cause had led to so much suffering as the consumption of alcohol.

Thus, as Lady Hope was a leading national figure in the Temperance Movement, it is certain that Darwin would have given her a warm welcome to his home at Down House.

Although Moore in his book, *The Darwin Legend*, contended that Lady Hope's account was a fabrication he did concede the fact that she had indeed visited Darwin, exactly as she claimed and indeed has suggested a possible date for the encounter. He points out that Lady Hope claimed that the visit took place, 'on one of those glorious autumn afternoons....he [Darwin] was gazing out in the light of one of those marvellous sunsets which are the beauty of Kent and Surrey'. On this basis and a search of the meteorological records he has put the meeting as having taken place between Wednesday, 28 September, and Sunday 2 October. I do not agree with this date for reasons that will be given later, but this is a minor point.

What is puzzling is that Moore has gone so far as to accept this part of Lady Hope's story, but not the details she gave of their conversation. One wonders what Moore imagines their conversation to have been. Does he think they spent the afternoon discussing the weather? She was an evangelist, and a very charismatic one, and was comfortable presenting the gospel to all types of people. She had worked with miners, lime-kiln workers, gypsies, thieves and thugs, and to those at the very bottom of society in the London slums. On the other hand, she was a member of the aristocracy and could speak to others of her class on equal terms. She had also mixed with the intelligentsia, and the clerical elite. For many years she had accompanied her father to the meetings of the British Association for the Advancement of Science, and had been introduced to many of the leading scientists of the day, including the very influential, William Spottiswoode, President of the Royal Society, and Printer to H.M. Queen Victoria.

Considering this background, the record of her conversation with Darwin does not seem out of place, the only surprise being Darwin's clear acceptance of the gospel and his apparent return to the Christian faith.

Moore contends that Lady Hope made up the story, and fabricated it so as to impress an American audience and to restore her self-esteem. It was all to do with 'self-aggrandizement' Moore declares. But was it? Did she really have to make up this story about Darwin in order to attract attention? I think not. The Northfield conference was a gathering of evangelical Christian workers, so for her to stand up and announce that she was 'a friend of Darwin' was surely not the best way of impressing them. If she really wanted to impress these people she would have told them a story about some of the other eminent Christians she had known. What about David Livingstone, or Dwight Moody? What about Florence Nightingale? Catherine Marsh, or General Gordon, or even Queen Victoria? The number of eminent people she had known is endless. This being so, Darwin must have been bottom of the list. Therefore, if this were an exercise in 'self-aggrandizement', as Moore contends, she made a poor choice of subject.

The only evidence Moore has produced to support his claims has been a couple of letters from the evangelist James Fegan. What is surprising, is that in these letters Fegan denied that Lady Hope had ever visited Darwin, a fact that Moore himself contradicts. In essence the letters, are a denigration of the character of Lady Hope, which is surprising in itself for Fegan was known to be a devout Christian of the strict Plymouth Brethren. This being so, I find it hard to believe that such a person would make a character assassination of a fellow Christian. Furthermore, there are a number of puzzling features of these letters.

Firstly, as I understand it, they are "reconstructed letters" that have been assembled by Moore, and an Open University colleague, from a copy of a letter written in 1977, by Mr. A.W. Tiffin, sometime secretary to James Fegan some fifty years before, and addressed to the Reverend A. Sowerbutts, of Southport, together with a recent typescript of several paragraphs contained in a carbon copy of a letter that had been dictated by Fegan in 1925. It all seems unnecessarily complicated, and it is difficult to understand why Mr. Tiffin did not supply a photocopy of the carbon copies dating from 1925. Although, I have not examined these documents, I do feel that the reconstruction of 'evidence' (if it merits that description) in this way would carry little credibility, and possibly it is on this account that Moore himself, in subsequent articles on this subject, has failed to mention this material.

Nevertheless, these letters do raise some interesting points. Assuming that they had been written by Fegan, and that their reconstruction is accurate, they make the following three main claims :

Firstly, Lady Hope's claim is a 'preposterous story' and is a fabrication. As far as he is concerned she did not visit Darwin and he did not return to the faith.

Secondly, that Lady Hope was a 'trial' to her second husband Mr. T.A. Denny. One letter stated: "Mr. T.A. Denny was an old friend of mine, and he gave me his confidence in the last year or two of his life – as to what he had suffered from Lady Hope. Indeed, it was the revelations that Lady Hope was running a River Club unknown to him that brought about his death! I presume that you know that, some years after Mr Denny's death, Lady Hope was adjudicated bankrupt." And again : "I do not think I overstate the case when I say that Lady Hope broke Mr. T. A. Denny's heart. The climax of her extravagance came when he discovered that, unknown to him, she was running a River Club. He went down to see it, and was seized with illness, which necessitated his lying on a water bed until he passed away."[40]

Thirdly, the letter continues: "When she was leaving here for America, she asked me to give her a commendatory letter to use in America, and I had the painful duty of telling her I could not do so."

With respect to this last claim, I find it difficult to believe that Lady Hope requested a 'letter of recommendation' from him. Fegan had very little social standing compared to Lady Hope. It was the year 1913, Britain had the greatest navy

---

[40] James Moore, *The Darwin Legend*, p.107-116

the world had ever seen, and Lady Hope was the widow of the Admiral of the Fleet, the principal naval aide-de-camp to the late Queen. Furthermore, she had standing in her own right. She was the daughter of a General. She had founded the Coffee House movement in Britain and was a successful temperance campaigner, and this would have made a significant impression on those people in America who were advocating stricter prohibition legislation. In addition, she was known as the author of numerous religious books which were being published in America at this time. For these reasons the claim that she required a reference from Mr. Fegan seems highly unlikely. Indeed, one only has to glance at the American press at this time to see that Lady Hope, even before the Darwin story surfaced, was welcomed everywhere she went in America, even without Mr. Fegan's piece of paper.

One further curious feature is that in one of the letters Fegan writes that he had, 'considerable uneasiness about her sayings and doings...' But her request must have been made in 1912, so what were the 'sayings and doings' referred to? It cannot be the Darwin story as this was not published until 1915, some three years later. There is no doubt that he may have had cause for complaint in 1925, but not in 1912, when he supposedly had received the request from Lady Hope. This does suggest that this comment has been made at a somewhat later date, so does raise serious concerns over the authenticity of these letters.

The second claim that she 'broke her husband's heart' and that she was in some way responsible for his death, is a very cruel and serious allegation to make. The statement that Mr. Denny was 'seized with illness' after visiting her River Club, and was forced to lie on a water-bed until he died is simply malicious. Firstly, the impression given is she was running some sort of Soho nightclub. It could not be further from the truth, it was the Connaught Club and it was for homeless men, and was run on strict temperance principles. Her husband was fully aware of the enterprise right from its inception as he had participated in its development. And as regards his illness being a consequence, this is ridiculous. Mr. Denny died on Christmas day 1909, when he was ninety-one years old. His death certificate states that the cause of death was 'cardiac syncope seven hours' and that he had died at Buccleuch House, Richmond. It is difficult to reconcile these facts with the claims made in the 'reconstructed' letters.

But they raise further concerns. The construction of the letters is somewhat unusual. Apart from the denigration of Lady Hope's good name, they give very little other information, and that which is given was accessible to anyone, and was readily available in published books.

In addition, there are some curious anomalies. Firstly, the writer refers to a recent issue of *The Tablet* which he had been reading. I find it difficult to believe that Fegan, a member of the strict Plymouth Brethren would have been reading this Roman Catholic journal, and more particularly taking any notice of what it reported. One is reminded of the naturalist, P.H.Gosse, also of the Plymouth Brethren, who was so anti-Catholic, that on visiting San Juan, on the coast of Puerto Rico, in the summer of 1846, he could not bring himself to enter the Roman Catholic cathedral, which he referred to as 'a popish mass-house'.[41] Edmund Gosse recalled how, as a child, he had been influenced by his father and 'loathed and feared' what they invariably spoke of as 'the so-called Church of Rome', which Gosse referred to as 'the Scarlet Woman' and Rome as 'the harlot's domain'. Edmund later wrote in his classic memoir, *Father and Son*, 'As a child, whatever I might question, I never doubted the turpitude of Rome... I regarded it with a vague terror as a wild beast...' It is therefore somewhat of a surprise to find that Fegan, a devout Plymouth Brother, (also a frequent

---

[41] A. Thwaite, *Glimpses of the Wonderful*, p.141

correspondent of Gosse) to have taken up reading *The Tablet* and being influenced by it.

Secondly, in one letter the writer refers to Emma Darwin as 'a devout Christian' and in the other as 'a sincere Christian'. Again, I do not think that a member of the Plymouth Brethren would describe Darwin's wife as such. It was well known she was a Unitarian, and even in the eyes of Darwin's atheist grandfather, Erasmus, Unitarianism was "a featherbed to catch a falling Christian". As a Unitarian does not accept the Divine nature of Christ, it is doubtful she would have been described as 'a sincere Christian' by a member of the Plymouth Brethren. One could again draw an analogy with P.H. Gosse, who caused a storm of protest when he refused to dine with a man on account of him being a Unitarian and as such had "denied the Divinity of my Lord".[42] Evangelical Christians would also have felt the same, one need recall Lord Shaftesbury, the leader of the evangelical movement, who in 1838, complained bitterly to the Prime Minister because a Unitarian had been allowed to dedicate a theological work to Queen Victoria.[43]

Finally, in one of the letters there is an intriguing postscript which asks the question as to why Lady Hope had not

---

[42] A. Thwaite, *Glimpses of the Wonderful*, p. 206
[43] J.L. and Barbara Hammond, *Lord Shaftesbury*, p.221

cleared her name from the slur of dishonesty made by Francis Darwin. Firstly, one wonders how the writer was aware of this accusation (as far as I have been able to discover) it had been made only in private letters, so how would he have been aware of it? Secondly, and what is probably the most significant point, would a Christian really feel the need to clear their name in a secular court. Is it not what a Christian expects, namely to have all manner of evil said against them. This attitude is somewhat surprising if written by a member of the Plymouth Brethren.

The upshot is that these 'reconstructed' letters amount to very little and as such are best dismissed. Even, if at some future date the original letters were to surface, and they were authenticated, they will still be of little value, for what they reveal is more about the character of their author, rather than anything substantial about Lady Hope. What is significant, however, is that Moore has largely based his case on this material, and as such has built a foundation on shifting sand.

Chapter 9

Six Good Reasons

The accusation that Lady Hope's account of her meeting with Darwin is a fabrication is completely unjustified and without foundation. Lady Hope was an evangelical Christian of the highest integrity. I am completely confident of this for the six good reasons given below, together with the conclusive proof of her honesty that is given in detail in the following chapter.

1. I believe she was a woman of absolute integrity

At the outset let us examine the biography of her father written in the year 1900. There is one story that is convincing of her reliability and it concerns a tortoise.[44] When she was a child she had travelled from India to Australia by way of Mauritius, where they stayed for some two months. It was while they were staying near Port Louis that they knew of a giant tortoise that lived in the area. She recalled that it was so large that three or four of the children could ride on its back, and it would carry them for long distances. In later life on relating this story she found many people to be incredulous of it and she began to wonder herself

---

[44] Lady Hope, *General Sir Arthur Cotton, His life and Work*, p.41-42

but then, "on reading Admiral Keppel's life the other day, I found the same tortoise not only spoken of, but exhibited in a drawing as it walked along carrying on its back six men. Thus unexpectedly our description was corroborated."

The fact that she was so concerned that this rather trivial story be corroborated indicates her complete reliability. In fact in all her writings she is very scrupulous to indicate whether a story was fact or fiction. For instance in the Preface to her book, *His Handiwork*, published in 1883, she makes this clear, she writes:

"The picturesque north country names, and familiar abbreviations of these, of many of the characters described here, I am obliged to dispense with, replacing them by more common and less recognisable ones. This alteration, however, is the only one [her emphasis] that I have ventured to make in these true stories. Otherwise every incident is definitely real."

In her book, *Loving Work in the Highways and Byways*, published in 1888, she gives the names and addresses of eleven individuals who were prepared to corroborate the facts she recorded.

In her book, *Heavenly Blossoms*, published in 1900, she makes clear, right at the outset, that, "In answer to the request of a few of my friends I have published some of the incidents which have happened to myself in that daily experience, which to every humble follower of our Saviour must ever, or may be, rich in the reception of..."

In the Preface to *Touches of real Life*, published in 1880, she writes: "This little book is neither nor less than that which it professes to be. Names of both persons and places are in every case fictitious; not so the incidents, the narratives, or the characters described." Whereas, in her novel, *A Maiden's Work*, published in 1882, she makes clear at the outset what it is. She writes: "I cannot claim for my story the virtue of rigid fact, neither can I call it fiction, for while most of the incident recorded is literally true, the blending together, with the names of persons and places, do not bear so high an origin."

In the Preface to her book of early memoirs, *Sunny Footsteps, or When I was a Child*, published in 1879, largely for the benefit of children [her 'little friends'] she writes: "I have ventured to offer to them this <u>true</u> account [my emphasis] of some of my early experiences, and hope that in reading my little book, they may have half as much pleasure as I have had in writing it."

In her book describing her experiences in the London slums, *Our Golden Key*, published in 1894, she writes (p.6) that, "My tale shall continue as it is – one of plain, unvarnished facts." And this claim is repeated throughout the book. Thus (p.95) she states again [my emphasis], "As this is a truthful account of facts..." and in case there is any doubt, she writes (p.79), "Certainly the histories before us read like a fiction, in some of their more tragic aspects; and yet they are literally and prosaically true, given just as they have happened, in their own natural lights and shades. There are no medium tints here. Everything is distinct, only too terribly real." And later in the book she describes the work of the tent missions to the Kent hop pickers she writes: "But perhaps it may be well to relate actual facts in connection with these tents, proving as they do, that the influences for good exerted within them are by no means transient."

From the above extracts it is quite clear that she would not relate a story to be true when it was not, particularly when a known person was involved. I believe it would be inconceivable that she would do such a thing. Furthermore, I am confident that the mere suggestion of this would cause her severe distress.

In an age when we read of much dishonesty throughout all levels of society, from the 'honourable' Members of the

Parliament, to the social security benefits cheat, we have lost sight of how brutally honest evangelicals could be a century, or so ago. To get some idea of this one needs to read Edmund Gosse's *Father and Son*, for in it we read of his mother, the evangelist Emily Gosse, who wrote hundreds of religious tracts, all of them completely true, as for her to 'invent' a story would have been sinful. Edmund Gosse recalled that his mother, 'had a remarkable, I confess to me still somewhat unaccountable impression that to "tell a story" that is to compose fictitious narrative of any kind, was a sin.' He then quoted directly from his mother's private journal, where she had written: 'I considered that to invent a story of any kind was a sin.' I believe Lady Hope would have felt exactly the same.

2. The denial of the Darwin family is unreliable

It is only recently that Emma Darwin's diary has become available to researchers. The year of interest is a small volume with the title page, '*Harwood's Diamond Diary with Almanack*'. In it one finds only brief notes and a simple code indicating whether she had had a good day, but what we do find is that she visited Mrs. Fegan on Monday 7 November 1881.[45] Mrs. Fegan, was the mother of James Fegan, and it is possible that Lady

---

[45] The Diary entry states: 'wrote Wm G. & Bessy, called at Keston & Mrs Fegan'

Hope was staying with her at the time of Emma Darwin's visit, so it is likely she received an invitation to visit Charles Darwin at that time, or possibly sometime shortly afterwards from Darwin himself. James Moore appears to have been unaware of the content of Emma's diary when he wrote, *The Darwin Legend* and has argued for Lady Hope's visit to have occurred somewhat earlier. I think he is wrong about this and that the visit occurred in early November. According to Emma Darwin's diary the weather at the time was 'v. warm', a fact confirmed from the reports in *The Times*, when the weather in the south of England was reported as being:

'very fine for the time of year,' Monday 7 November,

'The weather is fine and bright...' Tuesday 8 November,

'still mild', Wednesday 9 November,

'The weather is fine', Thursday 10 November.

Thus the weather being 'very mild and quiet' in the second week of November, would concur with Lady Hope's description, furthermore the glorious sunset she recalled would be more likely at the time of her visits (3 to 4p.m.) than a month, or so, earlier.

This date would also coincide with the absence of all the Darwin children from the house, so their denial that Lady Hope had ever visited their father would carry little weight. But what about Emma Darwin? She might not have told the children of who had visited their father. Visitors were coming and going all the time at Down House. Only the previous week they had entertained Miss Gladstone over several days to both tea and lunch, and another recent visitor had been Lady Mayne. Furthermore, Lady Hope may have been mentioned by her maiden name, Elizabeth Cotton, as she had been recently widowed and may have reverted to using her original name. Certainly in newspaper reports at this time she is still referred to as Miss Cotton. But probably a more likely explanation is that the Darwins already knew her as 'Miss Cotton', either from knowing her father General Cotton, or possibly from having come across her in Dorking as 'Miss Cotton', during one of their visits to either Leith Hill Place, where their Wedgwood relatives lived, or Abinger Hall where the Farrers lived, as both these places were very close to Lady Hope's Dorking home. Thus if she had been introduced as 'Miss Cotton' this would explain why the Darwin children were adamant that a 'Lady Hope' had not visited their father, without casting any doubt as to their honesty.

Lady Hope was also well connected. Her goddaughter Helen Evelyn, was the daughter of William John Evelyn (1822-1908) of Wotton House close to Leith Hill Place. Furthermore, she was a close friend of the Marchioness of Ailsa, and had recently been staying with her at Culzean Castle, when she had helped her run a Temperance tent at the Ayr Militia training camp. The Marchioness was the niece of the Duke of Argyll with whom Darwin had had numerous disputes over his theory. She would therefore have been cognizant of the evolution controversy and probably would have been only too please to meet its originator. Darwin, on the other hand, had a deep respect for the aristocracy and would have welcomed someone who had a connection with his old sparring partner.

As to the family's denial as to Darwin's conversation with Lady Hope, the fact is, they were not to know what he had said on this occasion. Other commentators have assumed that Emma Darwin would have also been present throughout the interview, as a sort of chaperon. But this is quite unlikely. Lady Hope's evangelism was always on a one-to-one basis. This is how she liked to work, and how she was able, particularly with men, to get them to open up and to express their deepest feelings. In her autobiographical novel, *A Maiden's Work*, she has her main character, Geraldine, almost certainly speaking for herself, when she comments as to her method of evangelism :

"I think I do better alone. I certainly never require any one there. The men are less shy when I am alone with them...."[46]

So it is likely that she was alone with Darwin for some time, and hence her record of their conversation becomes more credible. Although, it was the era of Victorian prudery, female evangelists seem to have been exempt from the propriety of having a chaperon. One only have to think of Edmund Gosse's account, of himself as a young boy, bursting in on his mother, the evangelist Emily Gosse, while she was alone with a soldier, he recalled:

"One of my vividest early memories can be dated exactly. I was playing about the house, and suddenly burst into the breakfast room, where, close to the door, sat an amazing figure, a very tall young man, as stiff as my doll, in a gorgeous scarlet tunic. Quite far away from him at her writing desk, my Mother sat with her Bible open before her, and was urging the gospel plan of salvation on his acceptance....This guardsman was in the act of leaving for the Crimea, and his adventures, - he was converted in consequence of my Mother's instructions, - were afterwards

---

[46] Lady Hope, *A Maiden's Work*, p.113

told by her in a tract, called '*The Guardsman of the Alma*', of which I believe that more than half a million copies were circulated. He was killed in that battle.....'"[47]

In which case, Emma Darwin would not have known of her husband's conversation with Lady Hope, and neither would the Darwin children.

However, it is quite understandable that the Darwin family would have wished to maintain and protect their image of Darwin. They wanted to preserve the authorised version as given in, *The Life and Letters*, that had been published by Francis Darwin. However, when they heard of Lady Hope's story, they overreacted with a vitriolic attack on her character in an attempt to squash the story. That they had overreacted is clear from the silly mistake Henrietta Litchfield made when she denied that there was a summer-house at the end of the Sandwalk at Down House.

3. There is a 'ring of truth' about Lady Hope's story

What is striking is that when Lady Hope's account is carefully scrutinized it is found to be packed with intimate details that could only have been obtained by an actual meeting with Darwin at Down House. Even Moore has acknowledged this

---

[47] Edmund Gosse, *Father and Son*, p. 54

fact and has accepted that the account, 'contains startling elements of authenticity'. Let us now look at these in detail :

(i) Her description of the view from Darwin's upstairs bedroom 'of a far stretching scene of woods and corn fields' is an accurate description and may be confirmed today on a visit to Down House, which is now looked after by English Heritage.

(ii) She describes Darwin as wearing 'a soft embroidered dressing gown of a rather rich purple shade' and this is a reasonable description, as he did wear a reddish-brown dressing gown which might have appeared purple in the autumn dusk.

(iii) She also describes accurately how when Darwin became excited that his fingers twitched nervously. This is known to have been how he reacted on these occasions.

(iv) Her account reports that Darwin had told her, "I have a summer-house in the garden...It is over there," he said pointing through the open window. Despite Henrietta's initial denial that there had been a summer-house, it is now agreed that there was one at the end of Darwin's Sandwalk, and that its roof was visible from the upstairs bedroom window.

(v) Darwin asked her to conduct a service in the summer-house for his servants and that he would be listening to the hymn singing. This also credible, as the distance from the house to the summer-house is such, that singing would have been audible in the bedroom with the window open.

(vi) The suggestion of having the hymn singing at three o'clock in the afternoon is also credible, as it was at this time that Darwin would usually have his rest in the upstairs bedroom.

It is reasonable to assume from the accuracy of these facts that she must have visited Darwin at Down House, just as she had claimed.

Although when Lady Hope related her account it was some thirty years after the event, we do know from her other writing, particularly the very detailed biography of her father, that she had an excellent memory, and could vividly recall incidents that had occurred some fifty years before. Thus in 1900, when she wrote this biography, she could remember incidents, about her father, that had happened in the year 1850, some fifty years before, which were, "as fresh in my memory today as when they happened."[48] And later, "It is not surprising, therefore that on my own mind these early memories are clear and strong."[49] [my emphasis]

---

[48] Lady Hope, *General Sir Arthur Cotton, His Life and Work*, p. 42.
[49] Ibid, p.157

And when she wrote her own childhood memoir in 1879, shortly after she had married, largely for the benefit of her goddaughter, Helen Evelyn, the daughter of William John Evelyn (1822-1908) of Wotton House near Dorking, who was M.P. for Deptford, she could recall vividly celebrating her fifth birthday, some thirty-two years before. Also, while she was in India, she encountered a German missionary (at the time she would be about 7 years of age) she recalled : "The old man imprinted a lesson on my sleepy little mind – for I remember I was very tired....which I have never forgotten." [50]

4. She stuck to her story for the rest of her life

What is significant is that Lady Hope stuck to her story for the remainder of her life. In the aftermath of the First World War she moved to the West Coast of America, probably for health reasons, and it was here that she made friends with a circle of Christians to whom she retold her story. They were so concerned that she had not documented details of the episode that after her death they wrote up what she had told them and signed an affidavit vouching for their confidence in her sincere character and reliability. This account contains some additional information. The most important being that she had had several meetings with Darwin (possibly up to four) a fact which is

---

[50] Lady Hope, *Sunny Footsteps or When I was a Child*, p.83

suggested in the original account as there are no introductions and there is a degree of familiarity. Furthermore, the language used in the original account indicates previous visits as in the following (my emphasis):

"I used to feel when I saw him..."

"...an open Bible which he was always studying."

"What are you reading now," I asked.

"Still Hebrews"

The possibility that there had been more than a single visit is confirmed by an intriguing footnote in a book written by Sir Robert Anderson (1841-1918). Anderson was the head of the C.I.D. at Scotland Yard and had been in charge of the 'Jack the Ripper' murder investigations. He was an evangelical Christian and had been a close friend of Lady Hope. In his book, *In Defence : A Plea For The Faith*, published in 1907, he stated the following:

"I may add that a friend of mine who was much with Darwin during his last illness assures me that he expressed the greatest reverence for the Scriptures and bore testimony to their value."

It is clear that the reference is to Lady Hope and the phrase 'was much with Darwin' confirms that there had been several visits.

The Los Angeles affidavit also has the added information that as a consequence of Lady Hope's original account, and of the Darwin family becoming aware of it, that she had received an unpleasant letter from Darwin's sons 'a very angry letter', which had distressed her, and prevented her from further publishing on the matter.

It was while she was in Los Angeles that she met her old friend, Commissioner Booth-Tucker, of the Salvation Army. Her late husband, Mr. T.A. Denny, had provided much financial assistance to William Booth and the Salvation Army, so they knew each other well. She also had her Anglo-Indian background in common with the Salvationist. He asked her to confirm the details of her story about Charles Darwin which she was happy to do. Booth-Tucker subsequently published the details in *The Christian*, much to the displeasure of the Darwin family. But, it was a further indication that Lady Hope was determined to stick to her story.

Then around the same time she received a letter from a James Bole, a professor of biology at Wheaton College, near Chicago who asked her to confirm her story to him in writing. In reply, she gave her fullest account providing further details, including the confirmation that she had made more than one visit to Darwin, and gives further detail of the upstairs bedroom, with its fine bay window and high ceiling, and with its door opening directly on to the landing. Further details included an accurate description of the entrance to Darwin's house, viz. "I was shown the large gate that opened on to his carriage drive". And that,

"It was at luncheon one day, that the lady with whom I was staying, said to me: Dr. Darwin has heard that you are here; and he would like very much to see you. He asks if you could come over this afternoon."[51]

Also, additional facts, such as the room 'had a fine bay window' which it has; and a 'high ceiling' which is accurate.

There is also more detail in the conversation. Darwin regrets publishing his theory, 'They went and made a religion of it.' And in making the request for her to hold a service in the summer-house, he asks that they sing not the 'old drony' hymns but the new Sankey hymns. This is not so unreasonable as he probably had heard these hymns being sung in Fegan's Gospel Hall at the bottom of his garden. However, she explains that there was never any service held in the summer-house on account of the Darwin family putting a block on it. Whether this was on account of Emma Darwin being a Unitarian and not

---

[51] J. Bole, quoted in, Moore, *The Darwin Legend*, p.88

wanting to encourage Lady Hope's form of evangelism is not clear. What is clear in this version of her account, is that the invitation to Down House had been directly from Darwin himself. Thus Emma Darwin's visit to Mrs. Fegan may have been incidental and not for the direct purpose of inviting Lady Hope to meet her husband. And this would possibly concur with Emma Darwin's lukewarm attitude towards Lady Hope.

5. There is independent support for her story

Support for Lady Hope's story comes from what we know about Darwin's servants. Francis Darwin has written that Darwin was reticent in discussing religion with his family, he recalled that his father, "spoke little on these subjects..." On the other hand, it may be that he could reveal his innermost thoughts more easily with a total stranger, such as Lady Hope, or possibly one of the servants. Darwin's family may therefore have not been fully cognizant of the extent of his conversion.

From Fegan's account, it is known that many of Darwin's household had been converted, including Mrs. Evans, Mrs. Sales and the old butler, Parslow. He had worked for Darwin for many years, and although he had retired in 1875, he still lived in the village and retained friendly relations with the Darwin family. It is known that in the spring of 1881 he was converted in one of Fegan's revival meetings. One of the servants who had helped nurse Darwin, in his final illness, has left a record of that time. We do not know whether it was Mrs. Evans, or Mrs. Sales. Whoever it was, it is known that she attended the Gospel Hall in the village, and many years later passed on her memories to a young man in the congregation. He was Mr. A.H. Nicholls who lived in Downe all his life and was a local tradesman. In the 1881 Census he is recorded as living in the Mill House in Downe with his father, Alfred Nicholls, who was the village miller and baker. Furthermore, we know from one of Emma Darwin's letters that the Nicholls family attended the Gospel Hall. The young Mr. Nicholls remained a member of the Downe Gospel Hall congregation, and is remembered as a man of integrity and a sincere Christian. Before he died in1957, aged 97 years, he passed on his recollections to a Mr. Leonard Fawkes, who published them in a letter to the *Bromley and Kentish Times*. This is what he wrote:

"Sixty years ago I was a schoolboy at Downe and the Darwin influence was still evident, chiefly through individuals who had been connected with Down House. Among those who had personal touch with the lady who had nursed Darwin was the late Mr. A.H. Nicholls, a local tradesman and a man known for his integrity and fine Christian principles. He died last year at the age of 97.

During one of my visits to him he told me that this lady who had been in attendance on Darwin prior to his death had informed him that he requested her to read the New Testament to him and asked her to arrange for the Sunday school children to sing 'There is a green hill far away'. This was done and Darwin who was greatly moved said: 'How I wish I had not expressed my theory of evolution as I have done'."

It is possible that the 'lady who nursed him' was Mrs. Evans, as she had been with the Darwin household as a nurse for many years, and as she was a member of the Gospel Hall congregation, she could have easily arranged for the Sunday school to sing an Easter hymn for Darwin.

This is an independent and separate account of Darwin's conversion. One can be confident that there has been no confusion with Lady Hope's account, for two reasons, firstly there is no question as to the role Lady Hope played and it was that of an evangelist and not a nurse, indeed at the time she visited Darwin he was not in need of a nurse; and secondly this lady actually communicated the story to Mr. Nicholls somewhat later, which would rule out Lady Hope as she moved away from the area, as well as the fact that she did not attend the Gospel Hall Mission. This is therefore, independent support, for Lady Hope's claim that Darwin had had a change of heart towards the end of his life.

6. Darwin's conversion is not surprising

What most biographers have agreed on is that Darwin was not an atheist, like his friend Thomas Huxley. Darwin could never have waged a holy war against William Booth's Salvation Army as Huxley had done. Indeed for most of his life he was largely sympathetic to Christianity. Indeed, for many years he had given financial support to the South American Missionary Society, and announced that he would be proud to be elected an honorary member. And we know that he encouraged James Fegan's evangelical mission in Downe village and provided him with accommodation in a building on his land. These were not acts that indicated he had completely discarded the faith he had had in his youth. This being so, I feel it would not be surprising if towards the end of his life he returned to that faith. Certainly he would not have been the first to do so.

Even in recent times there have been remarkable conversions of self-declared atheists. For many years, I had a correspondence with the atheist Professor Antony Flew, of

Reading University, so I know how the atheist can change when it comes towards the end. I was not surprised therefore to read his public repentance in the pages of the *Sunday Times* of 12 December, 2004, when in a full page article under the headline, **'Sorry, says atheist-in-chief, I do believe in God after all'**, the newspaper reported that:

"A LOST sheep has returned to the fold. One of the most renowned atheists of the past half century has changed his mind and decided that there is a God after all."

Then alongside his photograph, Professor Flew recanted and confessed: "As people have been influenced by me, I want to try and correct the enormous damage I may have done."

The following week the newspaper continued the story and declared that:

"Flew, professor emeritus at Reading University, is one of the most renowned atheists of the past half-century, whose papers and lectures have formed the bedrock of unbelief for many adherents."

And that after his retraction he had been, "denounced by unbelievers for stupidity, betrayal, senility and everything you could think of."

Much of this sense of betrayal probably arose from the publication of Flew's last book entitled, *There is a God: How the World's Most Notorious Atheist Changed His Mind*, published in 2007. However, he has not been alone in returning to faith, and publishing his reasons before he died.

Another notorious atheist to do so was Professor C.E.M. Joad (1891-1953) who was professor of philosophy at the University of London, and became a celebrity from being on the BBC's *Brains Trust* in the 1950s. In his day he was considered by the general public as the greatest philosopher in the country. From the BBC's studios he had preached his atheistic doctrines week after week, but then towards the end of his life he recanted and returned to the faith of his youth, and in 1952 he published an account of his journey back to faith in his book, *The Recovery of Belief*.

Why should Darwin have been any different?

Chapter 10

Truth or Fable?

We began this investigation into Lady Hope's account of Darwin's conversion to the Christian faith by examining some of her anecdotes and considering whether they were as she claimed real stories, or simply pious fables. Professor Moore is adamant that they do not represent historic events. They were just 'tall stories', and the Darwin story is just the latest in 'a string of fabrications'. Lady Hope's 'embroidery was exquisite', he claims, and the stories were 'shrewdly crafted'. As to the purpose he is equally as confident. It was all for 'self-aggrandizement' and 'colouring her own good deeds'.

It is understandable that Lady Hope in recording her experiences felt it necessary to maintain the anonymity of the individuals mentioned. Sometimes, she would use the first letter of the name, and on other occasions just the first name, and then she might invent a name, or a place, and usually explain that she had done so. This being so, it is now very difficult to track down and identify the persons, "Tall tales can be intractable, with anonymous subjects..." Moore has cynically concluded.

However, if this could be achieved it would substantiate her accounts, and so confirm that they were indeed true stories, rather than fables as Moore contends. Let us therefore look at one of her stories which on the surface appears an unlikely tale and seems to fit in with what Moore describes as, "the same old idiom used in her accounts of the dying miner and the depressed doctor. The bedside scene....the approach of death, the hope of salvation...all were authenticating marks..." The story, first published in 1876, is the account of two brothers who worked for the post office. It reads as follows:

"I shall venture to relate an incident which occurred at the time of the Prince of Wales' illness, now just four years ago.

It was on a cold morning in January that a telegram was brought to me. Finding the answer needed some consideration, I told the servant I would give the answer to the telegram boy myself when I had written it. As I handed the paper to him in the hall, it struck me that he looked very ill. An interesting face he had – dark eyes, so sad and anxious they looked today, pretty features, dark brown hair. But this morning his lips were white and trembling, and the poor hand he stretched out to take my missive looked thin and wasted. 'Is anything the matter?' I said. He nodded his head, but did not speak. 'You look very ill to-day; tell me all about it?' He took his little handkerchief from his pocket and shewed me some crimson spots of blood upon it. My look of distress brought the tears to his own eyes, and then they dropped hot and fast on his little uniformed sleeve. 'I've got such a cough,' he said, 'I can scarce walk up this hill' (alluding to the hilly walk which leads to our house) 'that's what's made the blood come, and now I seem so faint. How shall I get home?' And here his tears flowed very fast. 'But I must work.'

'Oh! No, my child,' I said; 'you are not fit for work, you ought to have a rest.'

'But mother's a widow,' answered the boy, 'and my five shillings a week pays her rent...'

And so the melancholy little figure passed out of sight, but not out of mind. He could not be so easily forgotten. In another hour I was at his home conversing with his mother on the subject of her sick boy. 'Which one do you mean?' she asked; 'they are both as ill as they can be.' And then I remembered that I had often noticed the little pair of telegraph boys, so much alike, standing at the door of the post-office. 'I will call them both in' she said; and there stood before me the two brothers, their short breath, deep incessant cough, and hectic flush, shewing all the symptoms of rapid decline. I begged that some arrangement might be made by which the two boys could obtain rest. Change of air they would not hear of...and so it was settled, by the kindness of their employers, that their places should be filled for a time.

In my daily visits to the boys, I used to find them seated opposite one another, propped up with pillows, by the fireside. A few days passed, and then they were laid side by side in a little bed, in the upstairs room.

One day on my arrival, the mother said to me, 'Willy has begun to think, from what the doctor says, that he shall never be well again – and poor boy! He seems in great trouble.' I went upstairs, and sat down by his bed-side. 'Are you not well today Willy?'

'Oh no! Miss, and it seems such a dreadful thing.' Here he covered his face with his poor hands, and then, looking round at his brother, he said, 'Yes! Arthur is asleep, so I can tell you – I think I am going to die!...Oh, do kneel down and pray – pray that I may get well...'

'I am going to tell you what God says, Willy. Believe on the Lord Jesus Christ, and thou shalt be saved.'

'What does that mean?' he asked.

'It means trust in Him, just as you trust your mother. Believe His word, just as you believe mine. I said I would come today, and you quite believed me, so you expected me. If you believe in Jesus Christ today, He says, you shall be saved'....The boy was silent for some minutes, and then he said, 'Thank you for coming today, and thank you for telling me. Thank Him too! Please kneel down and pray, and thank Him for all this good news.' As I knelt down, he said, 'You can tell Him I do believe.' I did so. When I rose from my knees, Willy's hands were clasped together, his lips were moving....

From that day Willy liked me to read to him about heaven and often said, 'I have no fear now, Jesus will be there to meet me; but poor Arthur, he will miss me so.'

A Silent Comforter hanging on the wall opposite his bed gave him great enjoyment. Each day he spoke of his 'text'....

At last the end was drawing very near, when one morning, as I entered his room, he said, 'Please read my verse for today.' It was this 'In all their afflictions He was afflicted, and the angel of His presence saved them.'... 'Saved them'.....I heard the feeble voice gently repeating these words as I went from his bedside at the close of my visit. On my return from London, where I had been spending a few hours the following day, the postman brother told me at the station....Willy had left us. The angel of a higher presence had called him away. Willy's last words had been, 'Saves me – saves me.'

And then was left a sorrowing household; but none so sad as his little brother. It was on that Saturday evening that I passed through the streets full of rough drunken men, boys at play, and groups of loudly talking idlers by the shop windows and the public house doors, on my way to visit little Arthur. I had been alone in the room with him for a few minutes, when he said, 'I want something – I want it very much. I want you to let me come to your house on the day that the men take him away. I couldn't bear to hear them taking him away. The child, as he lay there propped up with pillows, his breath so laboured, his white hand hanging feebly over the coloured dressing jacket which covered his wasted shoulders, did not look able for a journey; and yet I had hardly the courage to give even a doubtful answer to his earnest request. We talked about it together, and then he said, 'God answers us, doesn't He? Will you ask Him to let me go to another house that day when they come to take Willy away?' We did unite in making the request; and the answer was given to that little prayer...

Five days he lingered, slowly sinking away. One afternoon, as usual I called, and the poor mother said, 'He is very ill indeed. He won't know you...' When I went in, I saw indeed he was sadly altered....Looking up at the Silent Comforter, I read aloud the words, 'I know that my Redeemer liveth, and that He shall stand at the latter day upon the earth.' Two or three times I repeated over the little ear, now so nearly closed to earthly voice, the words, 'I know that my Redeemer liveth!'

The next morning was one of England's gladdest days. The bells rang out their merry chime and all nature seemed to join in the chorus of praise. It was our Country's great Thanksgiving Morning....But my heart ached for the little sufferer. So I wended my way to his home. 'He is gone,' said the weeping mother; this morning he was taken from us.....It was to have been Willy's funeral day,' sobbed the poor mother.

'Then Arthur's prayer is answered,' I said, 'and he has been taken to another house today.'

In the pretty cemetery shaded by its fine old trees, and overlooking the Mickleham valley, abundantly wooded there stands a little gravestone on which you may see inscribed the names of the two brothers, followed by Willy's verse : 'In all their affliction He was afflicted, and the angel of His presence saved them: in His love and in His pity He redeemed them.'"

This is really a very sad story, but it fits in to what Moore considers to be the deathbed scene, at which he claims Lady Hope excelled at relating. It was he claims, 'the archetypal anecdote, pathetic and plausible' which all evangelicals were happy to employ. Lady Hope had simply tapped into this 'huge voyeurs market'. I think this is a very cynical commentary for Professor Moore to make. The account Lady Hope has given is heart-rending and just reading it is sufficient to convince one that this can only have been a real life story. I cannot see how anyone could be so incredulous of Lady Hope's human goodness for her to have fabricated such a story. Her pathos is so tangible. Nevertheless, if one must scrutinize it, and subject it to historical criticism, so be it.

Thus, had it been true, or was it just a string of fabrications? Let us look at the facts. Firstly, we know the place. It is clearly Dorking, where Lady Hope lived with her parents, and the post office is mentioned. The only names are, Willy and Arthur, but no surnames. However, we can pinpoint exactly the chronology, for we know the date of the National Celebrations and Thanksgiving that took place following the recovery of the Prince of Wales from a dangerous illness. These celebrations took place on Tuesday 27 February 1872, when services were held at St Paul's and other churches, and it had been declared a public holiday. *The Hampshire Telegraph* on the Wednesday reported: "Yesterday was observed as a general holiday. The morning was ushered in by merry peals of bells from many belfries and continued at intervals throughout the day." This is exactly how Lady Hope recorded it, so we can be certain of the date.

From this one precise fact, I thought it might be possible, if the story is true, to identify the persons involved. According to Lady Hope there was a gap of exactly five days between the deaths of the two boys, and as Arthur had died on the day of the celebrations, that is 27 February, then Willie must have died on either, 22 or, 23 of the same month. I then searched the death registrations for Dorking for those dates, looking in particular for the deaths of males, aged between fifteen and twenty-five. I then came up with the names of Arthur Rowland, of East Street, Dorking, born in 1857, and died aged 15 years on, February 27, 1872. The cause of death, as stated on the death certificate was 'Phthisis'. And, William Edward Rowland, also of East Street, Dorking, born 1855, and died aged 17 years on, February 23, 1872. The cause of death, as stated on the death certificate was again, 'Phthisis'. Phthisis was the medical term used at this time to indicate tuberculosis, the symptoms of which are exactly as described by Lady Hope. Tuberculosis is extremely contagious so it is not surprising that both brothers contracted the disease considering that they both shared the same bed, a fact that is clear from Lady Hope's account.

I then looked up the family on the Census returns, and from this it was possible to establish that the boys' parents had been John Rowland and his wife Sarah. In 1861 they were living at Mill Lane, Dorking when the father was employed as a farm labourer. Unfortunately, the father died in 1864, so Sarah was a widow, and there were eight children, the youngest being twin boys, Henry and Alfred, born in 1862. The other children were, James, born 1846; John, born 1849; Ann, born 1851; Grace, born 1853; William Edward, born 1855; and Arthur, born 1857. I then looked up the family on the 1881 census when I found that the eldest son, James was indeed recorded as being employed as a postman.

Thus every aspect of Lady Hope's story was correct in all the details. The precise dates are exact, the mother was a widow, the older brother was a postman, and the deaths of the boys occurred exactly as related in Lady Hope's account.

The upshot is that Lady Hope did not fabricate this story, there was no exaggeration, nor embroidery. She didn't record it so as to "colour her good deeds", and neither was there any desire for "self-aggrandizement". This was an honest account of her experience.

In life, people don't usually change. The leopard doesn't change his spots. Lady Hope was completely honest in relating this story, accordingly I do not believe she would have changed in later life and on those grounds I believe that her account of her interview with Charles Darwin, in the autumn of 1881, must also be completely true and exactly as she recorded it in her statement published in 1915. This is what I personally believe, but others might have different opinions. Moore has claimed that "the noble lady passed a brilliant counterfeit" and he has been able to convince editors at both the universities of Oxford and Harvard to publish his view that Lady Hope was dishonest. He has achieved this, from his position as a professional historian, by promising to apply critical historical analysis to the account. "It is high time for historical criticism," he declared. "Time to scrutinize sources, tease out discrepancies..." and then as proof he illustrated his argument by giving an example of Lady Hope 'at work', he wrote:

"She climbs a narrow dingy staircase and enters a humble room. From his bed a dying miner reaches out and, seizing her hand, kisses it. 'I was wanting to see you once more,' he sighs. 'I have been very ill – yes – but it is all right. Jesus is with me. I cannot think much – no – but He thinks for me. Jesus is very kind. Oh! He is kind.' The man remembers his unchurched neighbours. 'Speak to them, speak to them,' he pleads, 'and have all the meetings you can.' The lady prays by the bedside, then bids him farewell, knowing they will be reunited 'at the Throne of Glory above!'"[52]

This was Moore's version, but if one looks at the original, one finds that it is very different. The original story is to be found in Lady Hope's book, *Lines of Light on a Dark Background*, pages 153-154. One finds that the incident had taken place at Carriden village, near to where Lady Hope lived following her marriage to Admiral Sir James Hope. The story actually reads as follows:

"I went to-day up a little outside stair, to see a man who is dying of a lingering illness. For many years he had lived as a bright Christian, following his calling as a worker in one of the coal-pits by the shore of the Forth. Working for his earthly living by day he devoted his spare time to the service of Christ. On Sundays, he was in the habit of teaching a large class of little children in a neighbouring cottage; and many an hour he spent in earnest interceding prayer for the drinking ones round him... When I came here, he said, 'May be the answer to my prayer for

---

[52] James Moore, in *Evangelicals and Science in Historical Perspective*, p. 225

so many years has come now; and the Lord is going to bless the people through your message. Speak to them, speak to them, and have all the meetings you can. God is sure to answer prayer.' Many a talk and prayer we have had together. I heard while I was absent[she had been away visiting her parents in Dorking] that he was much worse, and when I went to see him to-day, I found him far weaker. But he knew me well, and seized my hand and kissed it. Then he said, 'You have come back – just in time. – I was wanting to see you once more. I have been very ill – yes – but it is all right. Jesus is with me. I cannot think much – no – but He thinks for me. Jesus is very kind. Oh! He is kind.' One or two friends were there, and we prayed by his bedside, and thanked the Lord for the comforting assurances to the heart of His suffering servant. I may never see him again upon earth, but we must meet at the Throne of Glory above! This sick man has a deaf and dumb daughter, who talks to me on her fingers..."

Thus we find that Lady Hope was well known to the man, as they had known each other for some time before this incident. He was a devout man, and had spent all his free time preaching the gospel in the area, and teaching in the Sunday School. The dialogue, 'Speak to them, speak to them...' had not been spoken on this occasion at all. It had been spoken some time before on their first meeting, when the man was overjoyed to find that Lady Hope had moved to Carriden and was intending to preach in the area, but this is not apparent in Moore's version. Furthermore, she had been away and on her return she had learnt of his illness, and hence the visit, but she was not alone, as Moore's account might suggest. There were several people present including the man's daughter, and they all prayed at the bedside. These facts now make the story much more credible.

"It is high time for historical criticism," Moore claimed. "Time to scrutinize sources..." Unfortunately, for Professor Moore this meant further denigration of the character of Lady Hope, so that instead of searching for historical sources, as would be expected in this situation, he engaged in further character assassination. He presumably thought that the story was "intractable" as it involved "anonymous subjects". If so, he was wrong, for it has been possible to unravel this story and the result has completely vindicated Lady Hope of any exaggeration or fabrication.

To understand how this was possible it should be stated that the account is contained within the monthly letter, which Lady Hope sent to her friends at Dorking. The particular letter is dated April 1878, but in the letter she sent the following month the story unfolded, she wrote:

"This very week the one whom I mentioned to you in my last letter died, after having given glorious testimonies to the grace and power which the Lord can show in sustaining His people, even through long and lingering pain, and into the last dark valley. What must that meeting be beyond the shadow! At just the same hour another man died in the same street; but oh! What a different life! And where was the hope in his death?"

Although this story involved 'anonymous subjects' I thought it might be possible to identify the individuals and so substantiate Lady Hope's claims. In the first instance, I searched the death records for all the males aged between 30 and 75 years who had died in the parishes of Bo'ness and Carriden during the years 1878 and 1879. I then went through the records individually until I found two individuals who had died on the same day and lived in the same street. This was not as difficult as it might have seemed, and I was able to pinpoint the men involved. They both lived at Grangepans in Carriden, were of the same age, and had been coal miners. The first man was Alexander Bell, aged 61 years, who is described as a pitheadman, and his death is registered as May 13th and being due to 'asthma, dropsy, 12 months'. The second was William Main, aged 62 years, who is described as a miner. His death is also registered as May 13th and again being due to 'asthma, 12 months and dropsy'. Thus Lady Hope's story is confirmed, however, which man was her Christian friend? This was solved by looking at the census returns for 1871. Fortunately, the Scottish census return, unlike the English counterpart, contain additional information as to any disabilities, and in the 1871 census return for Alexander Bell it records that his daughter Jane Bell, aged 27, and occupation, dressmaker, was 'deaf and dumb from birth'. This is also recorded in the 1881 census when she was recorded as being unmarried and living with her widowed mother, Catherine. This fact had been given in Lady Hope's account so we can be certain that her friend had indeed been Alexander Bell.

Jane Bell, who was of similar age to Lady Hope, appears to have been an intelligent woman and one who, despite their differing social positions, had gained Lady Hope's friendship and respect. In her letter Lady Hope describes how she had copied out '*in the type-writer*' a short article entitled 'A short paper for the deaf and dumb' and had given this to the young lady, commenting that, 'I am sure she will be delighted when she has read it.'

Thus with careful historical scrutiny Lady Hope's story is confirmed in all the details, however, there is one further remarkable finding. This derives from the thoroughness of the

Scottish registration system, in that not only is the date of death recorded, but along with it the precise time. Lady Hope had stated that William Main had died 'just at the same hour' as her friend, Alexander Bell. And when we look on the registration we find that William Main had died at 2.30 pm and Alexander Bell at 4.30 pm, thus Lady Hope's account is accurate to almost the minute, which considering the circumstances, is remarkable in itself.

The overall conclusion is clear. Not only are Lady Hope's stories perfectly truthful, as one would expect of a evangelical Christian, but they are extremely accurate, which is not surprising when one considers she had been brought up the daughter of a General in the Royal Engineers.

Chapter 11

Epilogue

On Wednesday 26 April 1882, Charles Darwin was immortalized for all time by an official funeral in Westminster Abbey and laid to rest alongside David Livingstone and Sir Isaac Newton, to be amongst the nation's great heroes. Of the eight pall-bearers who helped carry Darwin's remains to his final resting place, three of them had some connection with Lady Hope.

There was William Spottiswoode (1825-1883) president of the Royal Society, who just a few months earlier, had entertained Lady Hope on the verandah of his country house, Combe Bank, at Sundridge in Kent.[53] She recalled that he was 'a very hospitable and kind host', however, it was not their first meeting, for she had met him at meetings of the British Association, on occasions when she had accompanied her father.

At this time William Spottiswoode would have been interested to have news of Lady Hope's father and his newly patented

---

[53] Lady Hope, *English Homes and Gardens*, p.159 (Combe Bank is today a Convent school for girls).

tricycle, as he had recently acquired one himself.[54] Also Lady Hope would have been welcomed to Combe Bank by Spottiswoode's wife, who like Lady Hope had an Anglo-Indian background.[55]

Secondly, there was the Duke of Argyll, who had over the years engaged Darwin in controversy. He was the uncle of Lady Hope's best friend, the Marchioness of Ailsa, whom she had recently helped manage a gospel tent in her temperance campaign in Ayrshire.

Thirdly, there was Alfred Russel Wallace, the co-discoverer of evolution by natural selection. He had been a close neighbour of Lady Hope while he lived in Dorking during the period 1876-78. During this time he had rented a house in the Rose Hill district of Dorking, which was just a stone's throw from Lady Hope's home in Tower Hill. It is almost certain he would have come across her Coffee Room in the centre of the town, and known about her gospel and temperance work, furthermore, he would have known about her father, General Cotton, on account of his famine prevention schemes in India.

---

[54] In 1882 Spottiswoode had a serious accident on this tricycle that contributed to his early death the following year.

[55] Spottiswoode's wife, Eliza Taylor, was the eldest daughter of William Urquhart Arbuthnot, a distinguished member of the Indian Council.

Moore has suggested that Lady Hope fabricated her story after having obtained intimate information about Darwin from those who had been acquainted with him. 'The more intimate titbits,' he wrote, 'might have been winkled out of members of the Darwin household'.[56] Lady Hope probably did know those members of the Darwin household that attended the Downe Gospel Hall, such as Parslow, Darwin's retired butler, together with other servants such as Mrs. Sales, and Mrs. Evans. As Lady Hope records in her account she was visiting homes in Downe village doing Bible readings, and almost certainly would have encountered some of Darwin's household. However, she had a much wider source of 'inside and intimate' information, for she mixed in the same social circle as did Darwin. She was acquainted with Angela Burdett-Coutts, who had recently organised a garden party for all of Europe's greatest scientists who were in London attending the International Medical Congress on vivisection at which Darwin had been given a place of honour. She was also well connected with Admiral Sir Bartholomew Sulivan, Darwin's close friend from HMS *Beagle*. She had shared a platform with him at a temperance conference and probably knew him well from her stay in Bournemouth. Furthermore, she was the widow of Admiral Hope, under whom Sulivan's son had served when her late husband was in

---

[56] James Moore, *The Darwin Legend*, p.54

command of the North America fleet. In addition to all this, she was friendly with Mrs. Fegan, with whom she stayed while she was working in Downe, and Mrs. Fegan was friendly with Emma Darwin.

Thus all these avenues would have enabled Lady Hope to obtain all the information she needed to fabricate an elaborate story, if she so wished, but such a suggestion is completely outrageous.

I do not believe that any decent person would conceive of such a deception, particularly a devout evangelical Christian. The fact is Lady Hope was a thoroughly good and honest woman. For her to have concocted her story would have been a complete denial of her entire life and contrary to everything she had ever stood for. And for what reason? What had she to gain?

Moore has suggested that it was for 'sensational self-aggrandizement', but he fails to provide any motive as to why she should have accumulated all the relevant 'intimate titbits' during the 1880s on the off-chance that it might become useful in the years ahead. At the time she was the widow of the Admiral of the Fleet, the daughter of a General, with a large circle of aristocratic and influential friends. She would have had no possible reason to think that one day, sometime in the future, she would be at rock-bottom in a foreign land and in need of a little puffing-up.

It is clear to anyone who has studied this matter (and even Moore has been forced to accept this) that Darwin did indeed invite Lady Hope to Down House in the autumn of 1881, some six months before he died.

Not many miles away from Down House the President of the Royal Society, William Spottiswoode had recently entertained her on the verandah of his country estate, why should Darwin have not wanted to do the same?

Indeed, Darwin had every reason to invite her, for he would have supported her gospel and temperance work in the area. Aside from this there is the naval connection. Darwin had spent five impressionable years aboard HMS *Beagle*, and he still kept in touch with old naval colleagues. These included Syms Covington, and Bartholomew Sulivan. Sulivan had been promoted to admiral and had informed Darwin that his son had served in the North America fleet under Admiral Hope. What could have been more natural than for Darwin, on hearing of the Admiral's widow being in the village, than he invite her to his home?

But they may already have been introduced. For many years Darwin had visited his sister, Caroline Wedgwood at Leith Hill Place, just outside Lady Hope's home in Dorking. On these occasions Darwin may have heard of Lady Hope's temperance work with the Coffee Room movement in the town. Then in 1873, Thomas ('Theta') Farrer, of Abinger Hall, near Dorking, a Permanent Secretary in the Board of Trade, had married Darwin's relative, Effie Wedgwood. From then on, the Darwins spent some weeks each summer at Abinger. A neighbouring estate to Abinger Hall was Wotton Hall, the home of the Evelyn family, and where the diarist John Evelyn (1620-1706) had lived. It is known that Lady Hope had connections with the Evelyn family for she was the godmother of Helen Evelyn. We also know from Emma Darwin's diary, for 4 June 1875, that the Darwins visited Wotton, so some connection is possible. However, one has to admit that a previous encounter between Lady Hope and Darwin remains only a tenuous possibility, but it is much more likely that Darwin was acquainted with Lady Hope's father, General Cotton. In the summer of 1877 Darwin had been staying at Abinger Hall when workmen had dug up the remains of a Roman villa. At the time Darwin was studying the action of worms in the earth, and he discussed his interest with his friend 'Theta' Farrer. Farrer was a keen horticulturalist and regularly exhibited at local horticultural shows. This being so,

Darwin must have discussed with Farrer the claims of his neighbour, General Cotton, who had developed a unique means of 'deep cultivation' that produced exceptional crops. Thus Darwin may very well have been introduced to General Cotton, and if so then his invitation to Lady Hope in the autumn of 1881 is not surprising.

In conclusion, if one accepts that Lady Hope had indeed visited Darwin in the autumn of 1881, just six months before he died, and as there is no reason to disbelieve her account of their discussion, other than the claims of the Darwin family, which are now acknowledged to be unreliable, then consequently one must accept what she has written, namely that at the time of her interview with Darwin, he had returned to the Christian faith. One could argue that Darwin was putting on an act to humour and please his visitor. But if it was all a sham, and he didn't believe any of it, why then had he invited her? Why, if he knew he was dying, would he go to the trouble to put on an elaborate performance? Furthermore, if it was all a pretence, why did he take it further and ask her to hold a gospel meeting for his servants? If Darwin was prepared to take part in this sham, for whatever reason, then it would reveal him to be a rather unpleasant and dishonest person, and this is contrary to all we know about him. I believe the only reasonable explanation is that Darwin had indeed returned to the Christian faith of his youth.

That he had done so is abundantly clear from Lady Hope's account as published in the Boston newspaper of 1915. It is particularly evident from the letter she wrote to Professor Bole of Wheaton College, Chicago, some five years later. In this she is more specific in her claims. She records that Darwin was devoted to the Bible, 'I never tire of it', and that he had come to accept Jesus as, 'the King, the Saviour, the Intercessor, dying, living...' These comments were not pleasantries but amount to a declaration of faith. Lady Hope was an intelligent woman she would not have inadvertently misunderstood these statements, however, it is clear from her subsequent statement that she sought reassurance from Darwin. When asked by him to take a Gospel meeting for the servants she asked him, 'What shall I speak on?' to which he replied most earnestly, 'Oh, on the Lord Jesus Christ'. What more confirmation would be needed to convince her that Darwin had indeed come to embrace the Christian faith?

Chronology

(Abbreviations : CD, Charles Darwin; LH, Elizabeth Reid Cotton, later Elizabeth Lady Hope)

1809   12 February. Charles Darwin is born Shrewsbury.

1825   CD studies medicine at Edinburgh University

1827   CD studies for Anglican Church at Cambridge.

1831   27 December. CD left England on board HMS *Beagle*.

1836   2 October. HMS *Beagle* returns to England at Falmouth.

1839   29 January. CD marries Emma Wedgwood at Maer.

1842   17 September. CD moves to live at Down House, Downe.

1842   9 December. LH is born in Hobart Town, Tasmania.

1854   LH and family leave India and arrive in England.

1857   LH and family reside at Hadley Green, Barnet.

1858   June.   CD receives Wallace's manuscript on evolution.

1858   1 July.   Joint paper presented to Linnean Society.

1859   24 November. *Origin of Species* published.

1860   30 June. Evolution debate at Oxford Museum.

1861   4 February. LH's father is knighted by Queen Victoria.

1861 20 February. City Banquet held in honour of LH's father.

1864 12 March. LH and father investigate Sheffield disaster.

1864 LH and family move to Bryansford, County Down.

1866 26 May. LH's father awarded the 'Star of India'.

1867 9 February. CD elected member of Missionary Society.

1870 LH and family move to Tower Hill, Dorking

1871 24 February. CD publishes *The Descent of Man*.

1872 LH opens Temperance Coffee Room in Dorking.

1873 5 August. CD visits Dorking (Abinger Hall).

1874 25 July. CD visits Dorking (Abinger Hall).

1874 August. LH in Scotland with Moody and Sankey.

1875 3 June. CD visits Dorking (Abinger Hall) and Wotton.

1876 1 June. CD visits Dorking (Abinger Hall).

1876 LH shares platform with Baroness Burdett-Coutts.

1876 LH publishes *Our Coffee Room*, an immediate success.

1877 20 August. CD visits Dorking and Leith Hill Place.

1877 6 December. LH marries Admiral Sir James Hope.

1878 10 August. CD visits Dorking (Abinger Hall).

1878 LH publishes *More About Our Coffee Room*.

1878   LH resides at Carriden and opens Coffee Room there.

1879   June. CD visits Dorking (Abinger Hall).

1879   August. CD visits Lake District and dines with Ruskin.

1880   15 April. LH speaks at Gospel meetings in Glasgow.

1880   6 June.   LH addresses large crowds at Maybole.

1880   26 June. William Spottiswoode visits CD at Down.

1880   LH is entertained by William Spottiswoode at Combe.

1880   28 June. CD visits Dorking (Abinger Hall).

1880   23 August. Hymns on the lawn for CD at Down House.

1880   30 October. LH with the Princess Mary in Edinburgh.

1880   November.   Admiral Hope taken ill at Carriden.

1881   February. LH opens new Coffee Room in Beckenham.

1881   9 June.   Death of Admiral Sir James Hope.

1881   22 June. LH's brother marries Marion Emma Heath.

1881   6 August. LH assists the Marchioness of Ailsa in Ayr.

1881   26 August. Death of CD's brother Erasmus.

1881   August.   LH settles her affairs at Carriden.

1881   28 September. Atheists Aveling and Buchner visit CD.

1881   21 October.   On a visit to Cambridge CD is taken ill.

1881   7 November.   Emma Darwin visits Mrs. Fegan in Down.

1881   8 November.   First visit of LH to CD, others follow.

1882   22 March.   LH shares platform with Admiral Sulivan.

1882   19 April.   Death of CD.

1882   26 April.   CD's funeral in Westminster Abbey.

1882   20 May.   LH gives farewell address in Bournemouth.

1882   4 July.   LH speaks to large audience at Regent's Park.

1882   September-December. LH helps with Moody and Sankey.

1883   LH does Gospel work in 'Outcast London'.

1883   LH helps with Moody's second London Mission.

1884   LH publishes her work on 'Outcast London'.

1884   September. LH addresses large crowds at Llandudno.

1888   21 March. LH addresses large crowds in Birmingham.

1888   10 October.   LH addresses large crowds at Wrexham.

1889   January.   LH seriously ill with influenza.

1889   December.   Death of LH's brother *en route* from India.

1893   27 September.   LH marries T.A. Denny in Paddington.

1899   July.   Death of LH's father.

1907   5 December.   Death of LH's mother.

1909   25 December. Death of T.A. Denny at Buccleuch House.

1911   LH declared bankrupt.

1913   LH leaves England for New York.

1915   August. LH attends conference at Northfield College.

1915   21 August. Publication of LH's account in Boston.

1919   4 April. LH makes her Will in San Diego, California

1922   22 February. Henrietta Darwin publishes denial.

1922   8 March. Death of LH in Sydney, Australia.

1922   9 March. Booth-Tucker confirms LH's account.

1922   7 June. LH's friends send affidavit to William Bryan.

1923   24 February. LH's Will proved in High Court, London.

1940   James Bole publishes LH's letter confirming her story.

Bibliography

Amos, C.W. Hale. 'Darwin's Last Hours', *The Monthly Record of the Free Church of Scotland*, February, 1957, p.33.

Anderson, R. *A Doubter's Doubts about Science and Religion, or In Defence : A Plea for the Faith*, (3rd edition) Pickering and Inglis, London (1924).

Anon. 'Temperance Workers: Lady Hope', *Methodist Temperance Magazine*, (1884) vol. 17, pp. 126-128.

Atkins, Sir Hedley, Down – *The Home of the Darwins. The Story of a House and the People who lived there*. Royal College of Surgeons, London (1974).

Barlow, Nora. 'Charles Darwin's Conversion', *The Scotsman*, 8 May, 1958.

Berra, T. M. *Charles Darwin. The Concise story of an Extraordinary Man*. John Hopkins University Press, Baltimore (2009).

Boulter, Michael. *Darwin's Garden : Down House and The Origin of Species*. Constable, London (2009).

Browne, J. *Charles Darwin, Volume I of a Biography, Voyaging*. Jonathan Cape, London (1995).

Browne, J. *Charles Darwin, Volume II of a Biography : The Power of Place*. Pimlico, London (2003).

Browne, Janet. 'Making Darwin : Biography and the Changing Representations of Charles Darwin', *Journal of Interdisciplinary History*, vol. 40, No. 3 (2010) pp. 347-373.

Clark, R. W. *The Survival of Charles Darwin*. Weidenfeld and Nicolson, London (1984).

Clements, J. *Darwin's Notebook. The Life, Times and Discoveries of Charles Robert Darwin*. The History Press, Stroud (2009).

Cochrane, Robert. *Great Thinkers and Workers*. W. & R. Chambers, London and Edinburgh (1888).

Cotton, E. R. (Lady Hope) *Our Coffee-Room*. James Nisbet & Co., London (1876).

Cotton, E. R. (Lady Hope) *More About Our Coffee Room*. James Nisbet & Co., London (1878).

Croft, L. R. *The Life and Death of Charles Darwin*. Elmwood Books, Chorley, Lancashire (1989).

Darton, J. M. *The Heroism of Christian Women of our own Time. What they have done and are doing*. W. Swan Sonnenschein (1880).

Darwin, Sir Francis. *The Life and Letters of Charles Darwin*. Volumes I-III, John Murray, London (1887).

Desmond, A. and Moore, J. *Darwin*. Michael Joseph, London (1991).

Drummond, Henry. *Natural Law in the Spiritual World*. Hodder & Stoughton, London (1898).

Evelyn, Helen. *The History of the Evelyn Family with a special memoir of William John Evelyn M.P.* Eveleigh Nash, London (1915).

Evensen, B. J. *God's Man for the Gilded Age. D.L.Moody and the Rise of Modern Mass Evangelism.* Oxford University Press, Oxford (2003).

Freeman, R. B. *The Works of Charles Darwin.* Dawson Publishing, Folkestone (1977).

Freeman, R. B. *Charles Darwin, A Companion.* Dawson Publishing, Folkestone (1978).

Fullerton, W. Y. *J.W.C. Fegan – A Tribute.* Marshall, Morgan and Scott, London (1930).

Gosse, Edmund. *Father and Son.* William Heinemann, London (1907).

Hammond, J. L. & B. *Lord Shaftesbury.* Penguin Books Ltd., London (1936).

Hattersley, Roy. *Blood and Fire – William and Catherine Booth and their Salvation Army.* Little Brown & Co., London (1999).

Healey, Edna. *Emma Darwin. The Inspirational Wife of a Genius.* Hodder Headline, London (2001).

Hope, Lady. 'Darwin and Christianity. A Remarkable Story told of the Great Scientist and author when he was approaching the end of Earthly life.' *Boston Evening Transcript*, Saturday 21 August, 1915.

Hope, Lady. *Invitations.* Drummond's Tract Depot. Stirling (n.d.) [1877].

Hope, Lady. *Lines of Light on a Dark Background.* James Nisbet, London (1879).

Hope, Lady. *Sunny Footsteps or when I was a child.* James Nisbet & Co., London (1879).

Hope, Lady. *Touches of Real Life.* James Nisbet & Co., London (1880).

Hope, Lady. *A Maiden's Work.* James Nisbet & Co., London (1882)

Hope, Lady. *His Handiwork.* S.M. Partridge & Co., London (1883).

Hope, Lady. *Gathered Clusters from Scripture Pages.* Macniven & Wallace, Edinburgh (1883).

Hope, Lady. *Our Golden Key. A Narrative of facts from 'Outcast London'.* Seeley, Jackson & Halliday, London (1884).

Hope, Lady. *Loving Work in the Highways and Byways.* T. Nelson & Sons, London (1888).

Hope, Lady. *General Sir Arthur Cotton R.E., K.C.S.I. His Life and Work. With some Famine Prevention Studies by William Digby C.I.E.* Hodder & Stoughton, London (1900).

Hope, Lady. *Heavenly Blossoms on Earth's Pathway.* The Christian Colportage Association, London (n.d.) [1900].

Hope, Lady. *English Homes and Villages (Kent and Sussex).* J. Salmon, Sevenoaks, Kent (1909).

Jackson, A. A. (ed.). *Dorking : A Surrey Market Town through Twenty Centuries.* Dorking Local History Group, Dorking, Surrey (1991).

James, P. D. *A Certain Justice.* Faber and Faber, London (1997).

Keith, Sir Arthur. *Concerning Man's Origin.* Watts & Co., London (1928).

Keynes, Randal. *Creation – The True Story of Charles Darwin.* John Murray, London (2009).

Litchfield, H.E. (ed.) *Emma Darwin – A Century of Family Letters* (2 vols) John Murray, London (1915).

Litchfield, R. B. 'Charles Darwin's Death-Bed. Story of Conversion denied.' *The Christian,* 23 February (1922) p. 12.

Livingstone, D.N., Hart, D.G., and Noll, M.A. (eds.) *Evangelicals and Science in Historical Perspective.* Oxford University Press, Oxford (1999).

Moody, W. R. *The Life of Dwight L. Moody.* Morgan & Scott, London (1900).

Moore, James. *The Darwin Legend.* Hodder & Stoghton, London (1995).

Numbers, R. L. (ed.) *Galileo goes to Jail and other myths about Science and Religion.* Harvard University Press, Cambridge, Massachusetts (2009).

Prochaska, F. K. *Women and Philanthropy in Nineteenth Century England.* Clarendon Press, Oxford (1980).

Raverat, Gwen. *Period Piece. A Cambridge Childhood.* Faber & Faber Ltd., London (1952).

Ridley, M. 'The God Squad and Darwin. Review of the book : The Life and Death of Charles Darwin, by L. R. Croft.' *New Scientist,* 13 May (1989).

Rose, Charles. *Recollections of Old Dorking.* (Reprinted from the West Surrey Times) Guildford (n.d.).

Secord, J. A. 'The discovery of a vocation : Darwin's early geology.' *British Journal History of Science,* (1991) vol. 24, pp. 133-157.

Sloan, P. 'The Myth of Darwin's Conversion.' *The Humanist,* March (1960) pp. 70-72.

Sloan, P. 'Demythologizing Darwin.' *The Humanist,* April (1965) pp. 106-110.

Spencer, N. *Darwin and God.* Society for Promotiong Christian Knowledge, London (2009).

Stone, Irving. 'The Death of Darwin'. *New Scientist,* 8 April (1982) p. 92.

Thwaite, A. *Glimpses of the Wonderful. The Life of Philip Henry Gosse.* Faber and Faber, London (2002).

Trollope, A. *The Small House at Allington.* Folio Society, London (1997).

Tucker, F. B. 'Charles Darwin's Last Days'. *The Christian*, 9 March (1922) p. 26.

Ward, Henshaw. *Charles Darwin. The Man and His Warfare.* John Murray, London (1927).

Wavell, S. 'In the beginning there was something.' *Sunday Times*, 19 December (2004).

Wavell, S. and Iredale, W. 'Sorry, says atheist-in-chief I do believe in God after all.' *Sunday Times*, 12 December (2004).

Williams, H. *Booth-Tucker, William Booth's First Gentleman.* Hodder & Stoughton, London (1980).

INDEX

(Abbreviations in this Index are: CD = Charles Darwin,

and LH = Lady Hope)